WASTE

Before you start to read this book, take this moment to think about making a donation to punctum books, an independent non-profit press,

@ https://punctumbooks.com/support/

If you're reading the e-book, you can click on the image below to go directly to our donations site. Any amount, no matter the size, is appreciated and will help us to keep our ship of fools afloat. Contributions from dedicated readers will also help us to keep our commons open and to cultivate new work that can't find a welcoming port elsewhere. Our adventure is not possible without your support.

Vive la Open Access.

Fig. 1. Hieronymus Bosch, *Ship of Fools* (1490–1500)

WASTE: CAPITALISM AND THE DISSOLUTION OF THE HUMAN IN TWENTIETH-CENTURY THEATER. Copyright © 2020 by Jessica Rizzo. This work carries a Creative Commons BY-NC-SA 4.0 International license, which means that you are free to copy and redistribute the material in any medium or format, and you may also remix, transform and build upon the material, as long as you clearly attribute the work to the authors (but not in a way that suggests the authors or punctum books endorses you and your work), you do not use this work for commercial gain in any form whatsoever, and that for any remixing and transformation, you distribute your rebuild under the same license. http://creativecommons.org/licenses/by-nc-sa/4.0/

First published in 2020 by punctum books, Earth, Milky Way.
https://punctumbooks.com

ISBN-13: 978-1-950192-88-5 (print)
ISBN-13: 978-1-950192-89-2 (ePDF)

DOI: 10.21983/P3.302.1.00

LCCN: 2020938428
Library of Congress Cataloging Data is available from the Library of Congress

Copyediting: Lily Brewer
Book design: Vincent W.J. van Gerven Oei
Cover image: Headlong Dance Theater, *The Quiet Circus: River Charrette 2* at Recycled Artist in Residency. Photo by Jillian Jetton. © Headlong Dance Theater.

HIC SVNT MONSTRA

Jessica Rizzo

WASTE

Capitalism and the Dissolution of the Human in Twentieth-Century Theater

p.

Contents

Introduction   15
    Prometheus Contrite • Existential Shame

1. Staging Capitalism: Dramatic Surplus and Inefficiency   29
    Dramaturgies of Waste • Failures of Sublimation:
    Harley Granville-Barker • Ibsen: "Life Is Work" •
    Policing Catharsis: The Passion of Politics and
    the Politics of Passion in Brecht • Postdramatic
    Theater/Postideological Theater • Wallace Shawn's
    Predramatic/Postdramatic Soliloquies • Elfriede
    Jelinek, *Regietheater*, and the Disposable Text • *The
    Merchant's Contracts*: Shoveling Shit

2. War: Abjection and Oblivion   71
    Heiner Müller, Hapless Angel • Revolution as
    Theater/Theater as Revolution • Elfriede Jelinek:
    Trümmerfrau of Language • *Bambiland* and
    the Society of the Spectacle • *Rechnitz* and the
    Exterminating Angel of History • Planned
    Obsolescence: *Death of a Salesman* • Phallic
    Coprophilia: Norman Mailer's *Ancient Evenings* and
    Matthew Barney's *River of Fundament*

3. **Crisis of Imagination: The Anthropocene**   109
Chekhov and His Discontents • "The Economy is the Crisis": Ibsen and Ostermeier's *Enemy of the People* • Despoiled Shores • Pathological Superiority: *Grasses of a Thousand Colors* • Posthuman Otherness • Rachel Rosenthal's Ecofeminism • *Stifters Dinge*: Posthuman Theater

4. **Debt and the Refugee**   135
Fassbinder and West German *Schuld* • Sarah Kane's *Blasted* and the Bedrock of Sexual Difference • *Charges*: Amnesty and the Unforgivable

Epilogue: *America*   161

Bibliography   163

Acknowledgments

This book is the consequence of many inspiring conversations and artistic experiments with cherished mentors, colleagues, and friends.

I am indebted to my long-suffering first advisors on this project, Paul Walsh and Magda Romanska. Magda also played a significant role in my development as a writer by inviting me to contribute to the *Theatre Times*. My meetings with Paul over the past eight years have sustained me through good times and bad, and I will be forever grateful to him for being my champion and my friend.

I have also benefitted from the models and mentorship provided by my other teachers at the Yale School of Drama. Catherine Sheehy, Jim Leverett, Marc Robinson, Gordon Rogoff, Tom Sellar, and Elinor Fuchs have all had a hand in shaping the way I write, the way I think, and the way I experience the theater and the world today.

Through my ever-challenging, ever-rewarding work with Robert Woodruff, I learned the importance of trusting my instincts, and the power of productive negativity.

My dear friend Ilinca Tamara Todoruț read and appraised an early draft of this project. She gave me the courage and the tools to make it the book I truly wanted it to be. I sincerely thank her, and sincerely look forward to returning the favor.

Phillip Wilcox assisted me with proofreading and citation management, for which I am thankful.

I have had the good fortune of working with many talented editors of both my scholarly and popular work during the years this book was in development. I learned from them all, particularly Karen Jurs-Mumby, Allyson Fiddler, Imani Roach, Gelsey Bell, Casey Beal, Cristina Modreanu, and the great Bonnie Marranca, whose own indispensable reflections are liberally quoted in the pages that follow. It has also been a great privilege to work with Eileen A. Fradenburg Joy, Vincent W.J. van Gerven Oei, and Lily Brewer at punctum.

Elfriede Jelinek's work is in many ways the heart of this book. I am immensely grateful to her, to her translator Gitta Honegger, and to my *Shadow. Eurydice Says* collaborators for giving me the opportunity to explore the possibilities of Jelinek's dramaturgy in real space and time. Mary Round, Kathleen Dimmick, Mollie Wise, Susy Brickell, Cho Young Wiles, Josephine Pizzino, Arianne Recto, Azusa "SheShe" Dance, Eloise Harris, Annie Dauber, Eli Green, Laura Petree, Lizzy Emanuel, Ariel Sibert, and Ashley Chang gave me their time and their faith, and I am beholden to them all.

I thank my mother Monica Rizzo for believing in the transformative potential of education, and for teaching my extraordinary sisters and I to be skeptical of received wisdom.

Finally, I thank Mark Lord for his steadiness, his gentleness, and his love.

In the beginning God created the heaven and the earth. And the earth was waste and void.
— Genesis 1:1

Introduction

In its clamorous polyvocality, T.S. Eliot's *The Waste Land* can be read as a variety of dramatic text — one with a dense, if dispersed, form that might have been unrecognizable as drama to readers in 1922 when the poem was first published but which would be all too familiar to twenty-first-century theatergoers acquainted with the bricolage dramaturgies of such playwrights as Heiner Müller and such directors as the Wooster Group's Elizabeth LeCompte. Eliot quotes liberally, in several languages, from sources ranging from Shakespeare to the Buddha to popular songs of the poet's day. High culture mixes with low. The sacred becomes entwined with the profane. Snatches of throwaway dialogue that could have been overheard in any bedroom or any bar come into conversation with the most exalted of utterances. No single, authorial voice unifies; the model of consciousness the poem proposes is a skittering one. It takes a step in one direction, then pivots before permitting itself to advance too far and sets off in another direction, only to pivot again. Insofar as each shift in tone or source text represents a foray into a worldview, avenues of inquiry are foreclosed nearly as quickly as they are opened. Eliot's grace and writerly poise collapse into a scrum of conflicting impulses comprising a self that fundamentally lacks confidence in itself.

The poem even struggles to end itself: "these fragments I have shored against my ruins," Eliot announces.[1] Language gets demoted to matter, to something with heft that can be defensively positioned between the self and the world. Language props up civilization. Language holds it all together and is now itself falling apart. The glue won't stick. The poet can't write, only pick up and rearrange the pieces.

The poem then concludes several times, rehearsing a mastery it never attains. Thomas Kyd's *The Spanish Tragedy,* "[w]hy then Ile fit you. Hieonymo's mad againe," suggests an acquiescence that truth, even if knowable, is uncommunicable.[2] Language cannot overcome this divide. Yet, Eliot chooses to quote *Hamlet*'s lesser-known urtext rather than the more iconic cultural artifact, which allows both plays to come alive in the reader's mind; the one invokes the other, and this invocation points to language's resilience, if not its efficacy. One play will close, one character will die, only to be resurrected and revised by some as yet unknown collaborator. The very impotence of language may speak across the generations, may create the continuity that sustains culture.

The penultimate ending, "Datta. Dayadhvam. Damyata," comes from the *Upanishads,* holy text of the Hindu religion, one of the world's oldest wisdom traditions.[3] In his notes, Eliot translates these words as "Give, sympathise, control."[4] Elsewhere, they have been translated as "give," "be compassionate," and "restrain yourselves."[5] In the *Upanishad* from which Eliot draws it, this tripartite admonition is broken up, delivered by the creator god Prajāpati to his three species of children: gods, men, and demons. Prajāpati repeats the same syllable, *Da,* three times, and his different categories of offspring hear, or interpret,

---

1 T.S. Eliot, *The Waste Land and Other Poems* (New York: Barnes & Noble Books, 2005), 81.
2 Ibid.
3 Ibid.
4 Ibid., 86.
5 Robert Hume, trans., *The Thirteen Principal Upanishads* (London: Oxford University Press, 1921), 150.

a different message. In this way, then, to the gods he recommends restraint. He urges the men to be giving. The devils he tells to be compassionate. Here is the hermeneutic that Eliot's poem demands; independently incoherent fragments, like nonsense syllables, cohere as different channels of expression in different readers' minds. Some early critics assumed that this was how Eliot imagined Sanskrit would be experienced by his readers, as nonsense, like Hieonymo's madness, a failure of language.[6] Madness and sacred knowledge appear as two sides of the same coin, irreducible, inextricable.

The final ending, "*Shantih   shantih   shantih,*" translates as "inner peace," or "the peace which passeth all understanding."[7] This cacophonous poem with its many borrowings, interruptions, and eruptions ends with surrender to the unsayable, an acknowledgement that that worth having, or being, cannot be told, cannot be wrangled into language. Solace is ultimately found in the mute void.

The Waste Land was initially praised for its "positive" content, its revitalizing transposition of Christian symbols and the Grail quest legend into a complex and distinctly modern idiom. Eliot encouraged such readings, announcing in his notes that the "plan" of the poem and "a good deal of the incidental symbolism" was suggested to him by a book on the Grail legend.[8] It was not until much later in the century that the poem began to be appreciated for that which had inspired censure upon its publication: its "negative" content. In 1982, for example, Eloise Knapp Hay described *The Waste Land* as "a poem of radical doubt and negation, urging that every human desire be stilled except the desire for self-surrender, for restraint, and for peace."[9] Read negatively, the poem becomes eloquent as a fresh disavowal of the species responsible for the First World War, which officially

---

6   Cleanth Brooks, *Modern Poetry and the Tradition* (Chapel Hill: University of North Carolina Press, 1939), 165.
7   Eliot, *The Waste Land,* 81.
8   Ibid., 82.
9   Eloise Knapp Hay, *T.S. Eliot's Negative Way* (Cambridge: Harvard University Press, 1982), 48.

ended just four years before *The Waste Land* was published. The war decimated the population of Europe, Eliot's adopted home, and revealed a hitherto inconceivable capacity for human self-destruction. The war also turned great swaths of the cities and fields of the continent into literal wastelands, barren and uninhabited by any save the fallen and the bereaved. In his poem, Eliot marshals great reserves of erudition to help him confront the catastrophe of the war, as if surely one of the many books in his eclectic library must contain the key to redeeming the carnage by rendering it meaningful. He fails. When the poem ends, a new kind of creature has been born — one which must live with the knowledge that its existence is irredeemable.

The First World War was one of two catastrophes that occasioned the writing of *The Waste Land*. The second was personal for Eliot; the poet suffered what was diagnosed as a nervous breakdown shortly after the war ended. Then-popular theories of "psychic scarcity" held that a person's supply of nervous energy was finite, like one's bank account balance. If they were not careful, psychic "wastrels" could overdraw and go bankrupt.[10] Unscrupulous, irresponsible, seen as menaces to themselves and burdens to others, wastrels of any kind were, then as now, not regarded as exemplary members of a society that cherishes productivity and efficiency. Eliot, who worked in a bank throughout the period when he was writing much of his most important work, and who frequently complained to friends and family in his letters that he was anxious about his personal finances, was initially prescribed a "rest cure" in a resort town on the southern coast of England to repair the damage he had done to his psychic bank account.[11] This treatment proved unsuccessful.

Instead, Eliot found relief under the care of the "psychological doctor" Roger Vittoz at a sanitarium in Lausanne, Switzer-

---

10 T.J. Jackson Lears, *No Place of Grace: Anti-Modernism and the Transformation of American Culture 1880–1920* (New York: Pantheon, 1981), 52–53.

11 Matthew K. Gold, "The Expert Hand and the Obedient Heart: Dr. Vittoz, T.S. Eliot, and the Therapeutic Possibilities of *The Waste Land*," *Journal of Modern Literature* 23, nos. 3–4 (Summer 2000): 521–22.

land. He also composed much of *The Waste Land* there. Though Eliot always professed an aversion to Freudian theory, Vittoz's methods were not in most respects too distinct from those of the originator of psychoanalysis.[12] Vittoz had his quirks — he believed that a skilled physician could detect the precise workings of a patient's brain by placing his hand on the patient's forehead — but his work with Eliot involved regular daily sessions and the pursuit of what could be understood as a version of the talking cure.

Vittoz also shared with Freud an understanding of the human psyche as an economic system, "a system for the production, distribution, and consumption of psychic resources."[13] From Lausanne, Eliot wrote to his brother, "[t]he great thing I am trying to learn is how to use all my energy without waste, to be *calm* when there is nothing to be gained by worry, and to concentrate without effort."[14] It is interesting to consider the title of *The Waste Land* in this light — Eliot was emphatic in letters to Ezra Pound and others that the title of his poem was not *The Wasteland*, which would have circumscribed its resonances, but *The Waste Land*. The former evokes a decimated, barren, or overgrown landscape, but the latter is a different way of writing "place of waste," which suits a text that doubled as a repository for what its author was being trained to recognize as his profitless worries, his failures to keep calm, his failures to channel his energy efficiently.

From the beginning, the narrator of *The Waste Land* wrestles with the inefficient complexities of his experience of himself and the world:

12 Bill Goldstein, *The World in Two: Virginia Woolf, T.S. Eliot, D.H. Lawrence, E.M. Forster, and the Year That Changed Literature* (New York: Henry Holt, 2017), 44–45.
13 Suzanne Raitt, "Psychic Waste: Freud, Fechner, and the Principle of Constancy," in *Culture and Waste: The Creation and Destruction of Value*, eds. Gay Hawkins and Stephen Muecke (New York: Rowman & Littlefield Publishers, 2002), 73.
14 T.S. Eliot in a letter to Henry Eliot, December 13, 1921, *The Letters of T.S. Eliot, Volume I: 1898–1922*, ed. Valerie Eliot (San Diego: Harcourt Brace Jovanovich, 1988), 493.

> April is the cruelest month, breeding
> Lilacs out of the dead land, mixing
> Memory and desire, stirring
> Dull roots with spring rain.[15]

The narrator gives the impression that he prefers the less ambiguous seasons — winter, summer — those that encourage *either* the dormancy of forgetting and abandonment or the tickle of surprise and discovery. April pulls in two directions; the narrator at once yearns to lie with the dead and to writhe in the arms of someone warm and new. The pull of mourning is overwhelming in *The Waste Land*. The earth is stony; abortion renders wombs barren and women prematurely old; Shakespeare's Ariel keeps singing, "those are pearls that were his eyes."[16] Here, as in the "neurotic" analysand, the psychic economy is an inefficient one, producing excessive, unwanted, and disruptive stimuli: psychic waste. The past interferes with the present and the death drive vies with the pleasure principle for dominance. Like Freud, Vittoz understood himself as being in the business of waste management, of helping his patient regain psychic equilibrium and constancy, where it was presumed something like health could be found. *The Waste Land* is also a record of its author coming to terms with the realization that, to exist in the modern world outside the confines of the sanitarium, the "worry," the perverse desire, the psychic waste had to be jettisoned. The world had become too much. The only way to survive it was to pass over the great majority of its sorrows in silence, to learn to ignore the insupportable violence at its foundation. *Shantih shantih shantih.*

---

15 Eliot, *The Waste Land and Other Poems*, 65.
16 William Shakespeare, *The Tempest*, ed. Stanley Wells et al. (New York: Penguin Books, 2007), 1:2:402.

Prometheus Contrite

Eliot's painful document of becoming-modern (or becoming-"well") is evidence that human existence is as bound up with what we discard, abject, and devalue as it is with what we recognize and revere. The narrator oscillates between a quasi-religious faith in language, in expression, in art, and in being ashamed of these superfluities of consciousness the way one is ashamed of the stench of one's own waste products. *The Waste Land* suggests that the most salient feature of being human is our ability to be ashamed of ourselves.

While late-capitalist modernity applies a new and terrible pressure to this existential fact, this is not a uniquely modern insight — it was articulated in some of our earliest aesthetic artifacts. Georges Bataille reads the first known artistic gesture as a negative gesture, an act of self-abnegation. Examining the prehistoric cave paintings at Lascaux, Bataille observes that while their early human creators rendered animal subjects with apparent reverence and relative anatomical exactitude, when it came to depicting human subjects, themselves, the painters omitted their own faces, and in some cases replaced them with the faces of animals.[17]

The painters omitted this signifier of that which is most elevated in the species, the organ of speech, individuation, and recognition. The painters rendered the human not as a superior and distinct entity capable of foresight, collaboration, and construction, but as a frail body among stronger bodies. "He had not yet prevailed," Bataille writes of man, "but he apologized."[18] Long before the human had acquired the ability to shape the landscape according to its vision and will, Bataille sees these early artists recoiling from the possibility that the human might come to stand outside of nature.

---

17 Georges Bataille, *The Cradle of Humanity: Prehistoric Art and Culture*, trans. Stuart Kendall (New York: Zone Books, 2005), 57–80.
18 Ibid., 80.

Hannah Arendt identifies this ability as the domain of *homo faber,* or "man the maker," the human animal engaged in work as opposed to mere labor. For Arendt, labor encompasses the biologically dictated activities necessary for subsistence; its products are consumed as quickly as they are brought forth. Work, however, refers to the fabrication of things designed to outlive their creator. *Homo faber* is the deviser of laws and institutions, the architect of cities, and the maker of art. Where the animal is of its environment, constrained by its horizons, *homo faber* takes the environment as a starting point. *Homo faber* moves through the world making improvements, revisions, shaping the world to suit her purposes rather than always only adjusting herself to suit the purposes of the world. The trees are there to be converted into timber, the water to be diverted, the surface to be adorned.

The prehistoric human could not have dreamed of industrialization, world war, and climate change, but she intuited the downfall that this initial separation would bring. According to Bataille, the Lascaux paintings represent "a stupefying negation of man. Far from seeking to affirm humanity against nature, man, born of nature, here voluntarily appears as a kind of waste."[19] Early humans perceived and depicted themselves as *waste,* as excess, more like a tumor in the flesh of the world than like the "masters and possessors of nature."[20] At the very moment when the capacity for image-making, for art, was emerging, the human felt not pride, but shame. The birth of this difference did not bode well—this difference carried within it the possibility of total annihilation.

This intuition, that our distinction would be as much a source of suffering as of joy, also motivates some of our foundational dramatic texts. The eponymous protagonist of Aeschylus's *Prometheus Bound* is a Titan who steals fire from heaven and gives it to human beings. His offense is grave not merely because he

---

19 Ibid., 46.
20 René Descartes, *Discourse on Method and Meditations* (New York: The Liberal Arts Press, 1960), 45.

has taken from the gods, but because Prometheus "gave honors to mortals beyond what was just."[21] In Aeschylus's telling, when Zeus ascended to the throne of Mount Olympus, he determined that the best thing to do with "the unhappy breed of mankind" would be "to blot the race out and create a new."[22] Prometheus alone, harboring a special fondness for the creatures, took pity on humans and saved them from obliteration by sharing with humankind "the brightness of fire that devises all."[23] Prometheus upsets the cosmic order of things; it is not for the human, frail and finite creature, to strive to create that which will endure. Zeus perceives the human's progression towards becoming *homo faber* as an abomination. Prometheus is admonished for giving that which belongs to the gods "to creatures of a day."[24] The god's anger is not mere jealousy. He knows the human's new aspirations are rooted in a dangerous lie because Prometheus committed more than one offense. Before giving human beings fire, he "stopped mortals from foreseeing doom," and "sowed in them blind hopes."[25] This original folly, which provides the scaffolding for our major narratives of human overreach — the Faust plays, the Frankenstein story — leaves the human fundamentally deluded about her nature and bound to suffer endless torment as a result.

As is Prometheus, who spends the play nailed to a rock, where he is condemned to remain for all eternity as punishment for his transgression. As visitors come and go, he bemoans his fate and attempts to justify his actions to whomever will listen. The play becomes a recitation of humanity's accomplishments as Prometheus tries to make the case for his betrayal. From his perspective, Prometheus has given humanity a great gift. He found mortals "mindless / and gave them minds, made them

---

21 Aeschylus, "Prometheus Bound," in *Greek Tragedies*, eds. David Grene and Richmond Lattimore (Chicago: University of Chicago Press, 1991), 1:66.
22 Ibid., 1:74.
23 Ibid., 1:65.
24 Ibid., 1:100.
25 Ibid., 1:74.

masters of their wits," he says.[26] "First they had eyes but had no eyes to see, / and ears but heard not. Like shapes within a dream / they dragged through their long lives and muddled all, / haphazardly."[27] Prometheus describes human beings living "beneath the earth like swarming ants / in sunless caves."[28] They groped their way through life, at the mercy of nature, incapable of design, unable to impose their will on their surroundings. Prometheus tutored them in the ways of *homo faber* — he taught them how to read the stars, how to domesticate animals, how to prophesy. Prometheus gave mortals arithmetic, written language, medicine, and the natural sciences. He set civilization in motion, and saved mortals from oblivion.

Or so he claims. One of Prometheus's interlocutors, the god Hermes, listens to the Titan's raving and, perhaps not incorrectly, concludes he has gone mad. Prometheus is a hero, but a tragic one, fatally flawed by hubris. *Prometheus Bound* is an atypical Greek tragedy in that it is almost entirely static — Prometheus is being bound by servants of Zeus at the beginning of the play and remains bound until the play's end. We witness neither an action nor a fall from great heights; we only hear about the hero's deeds after misfortune finds him. Prometheus's static position suggests that the fall of real consequence takes place elsewhere, that his personal fall is somehow incidental to the tragedy. The fall is humanity's to take. Prometheus has indeed given mortals a gift, but it is a mixed blessing. He has endowed mortals with hubris to rival his own, setting civilization up for a long rise and eventual fall, the denouement of which we now appear to be approaching. *Prometheus Bound* is believed to have been the first play in a trilogy. Of the other two plays, only a few fragments of the former, *Prometheus Unbound,* remain. In these, Prometheus finds himself subjected to fresh torments; a bird of prey visits him each day to peck at and feed upon his liver, which regenerates each night so that the bird returns hungry for more

26 Ibid., 1:81.
27 Ibid., 1:82.
28 Ibid.

every morning. The play that depicted Prometheus's ultimate triumph over his circumstances and reconciliation with Zeus, *Prometheus the Firebearer*, has been, appropriately, lost to history altogether. All we have are scenes of suffering; redemption is indefinitely deferred.

Of all the art forms, the theater is best suited to representing the human's perverse relation to her finitude. Each night, the theater calls into being a new and wholly unnecessary world at great physical, material, and emotional expense to all involved. As Tolstoy put it, when taking into account the farthest-flung and most tangential of contributors, every production "requires the intense effort of thousands and thousands of people, working forcedly at what are often harmful and humiliating tasks."[29] People literally destroy themselves out of devotion to the theater: "these people, often very kind, intelligent, capable of every sort of useful labour, grow wild in these exceptional, stupefying occupations and become dull to all serious phenomena of life, one-sided and self-complacent specialists, knowing only how to twirl their legs, tongues or fingers."[30] This labor is real, not infrequently all-consuming to the point of being disfiguring, and yet its products are ephemeral. The world of the play melts into air when the curtain falls. The baseless fabric of the vision dissolves, the insubstantial pageant fades. "We are such stuff / As dreams are made on," the theater reminds us in ritual form if not always in content, "and our little life / Is rounded with a sleep."[31]

In the theater, even our mightiest incursions into the void are, self-confessedly ineffectual, doomed before they begin. The stage is always already anticipating being cleared to make space for the next show to load in. The actor playing Oedipus adopts a part which is not really his, struggles as if the stakes were high. He curses the gods for casting a shadow over his existence with their prophecy that he would come to ruin. He curses himself for

---

29 Leo Tolstoy, *What Is Art?*, trans. Richard Pevear and Larissa Volokhonsky. (New York: Penguin Books, 1995), 9.
30 Ibid., 4
31 Shakespeare, *The Tempest*, 4.1.156–58.

the hubris that led him to believe he could root out the source of his people's suffering, that led him to disregard all warnings, led him to trust that knowledge would elevate him and allow him to attain mastery, when in the end it would only lay him low. For Oedipus, like the actor playing him, like the thousands of people toiling at their often harmful and humiliating tasks to bring the production to fruition, an illusion constitutes the substrate of his endeavor.

Everything about the theater is suffused with existential shame: the painted flats done up to resemble stone parapets, the cognac conjured from iced tea, the shabby, worn-out costume that only makes the actress appear elegant from a distance, under the lights, if she keeps her back to the audience so no one sees she is being held together at the waist with safety pins. And yet, how wasteful, how extravagant the theater is, a diversion of so many resources to be consumed in the blaze of a single performance before, more often than we might like to admit, fewer people in the audience than there are on stage. The theater is that rare and strange human accomplishment that understands itself as being made by and for "creatures of a day." At its best, the theater is not deluded about its nature, origins, and destiny. At its best, the theater gathers artists and audience in one space to die together for a little while, to consciously waste, not spend, their time.

Existential Shame

For Bataille, the principle of waste, or "nonproductive expenditure," steers all human feeling and behavior inexorably towards inefficiency and extravagance. Knowing on the deepest level, like prehistoric humans, that we *are* waste, we are paradoxically compelled to self-effacement through excess. Play, religion, eroticism, forgiveness, art; none of these human activities are *necessary* for survival, but they are what make life worth living even though (or because) they are not profitable in any conventional or measurable way. To measure the success or failure of these pursuits according to their efficiency or productivity would be to miss the point entirely. The effort they require is inherently valuable, pleasurable, meaningful. We cannot give back the fire; the question that remains is what we will do with it before the fire burns out.

Under capitalism, however, "everything conspires to obscure the basic movement that tends to restore wealth to its function, to gift-giving, to squandering without reciprocation," Bataille argues.[32] Under capitalism, the expectation is that any outlay should yield a return on one's investment, even though to be authentically human is to operate at a loss. Capitalism encourages spiritual miserliness, when human beings derive pleasure, honor, and glory, from freely spending their resources and themselves. "The more costly the life-generating processes are," he writes, "the more squander the production of organisms has required, the more satisfactory the operation is. The principle of producing at the least expense is not so much a human idea as a narrowly capitalist one (it makes sense only from the viewpoint of the incorporated company)."[33] Societies that privilege the acquisition and accumulation of wealth over its disbursal and consumption are sick societies. Bataille points to the potlatch ceremonies of certain Native American tribes of the Pacific Northwest as archetypical of the righteous squandering he sees as innate to the human. At these opulent feasts, tribal leaders would compete by attempting to outdo one another in extravagant gift-giving. He who divested himself of the most possessions would accrue the most prestige in his community. Our current economic system, however, privileges accumulation, parsimony, and the obsessive tabulation of debts, all of which, Bataille contends, contribute to the gradual mutilation of the human essence.

The theater is where we can see this most clearly. The theater is a waste. The theater is a prodigious waste of time and space. It is also, almost without exception, a waste of money for both

---

[32] Georges Bataille, *The Accursed Share*, trans. Robert Hurley (New York: Zone Books, 1991), 1:38.
[33] Ibid., 2:85.

producer and consumer. The ticket-buyer is not able to gather up the production and hang it on her wall if she finds it to be to her taste. Her purchase is gone before she has received the full benefit of it, and it has no resale value. The overwhelming majority of theater-making must be subsidized by funds derived from the state or other forms of patronage, and the theater would be decimated in a truly free market. The theater cannot save us. It cannot even meaningfully shape public discourse, so unequivocally marginal is the place theater occupies in our culture. Most people never go to the theater at all. And yet, for those afflicted with, or attuned to, the existential shame the theater specializes in, the theater is where we must go to rehearse our catastrophes, to atone for our excesses and our penury. "Vanity of vanities," the theater is where we go to be recalled to an awareness that "all is vanity."[34]

---

34 Ecclesiastes 1:2.

1

Staging Capitalism: Dramatic Surplus and Inefficiency

As in individual organisms, the growth of capitalist societies is sustained by consumption and the attendant production of waste. Unlike individual organisms, capitalism in its present state is built on the unsustainable fantasy of *infinite* growth. According to Marx, waste is not incidental to capitalism, but constitutive — capitalism depends on the existence of a "surplus" or "redundant" population of workers, a reserve army of the able-bodied but unemployed.[1] This surplus population allows for the extraction of "surplus labor," or the measure of labor that exceeds what the individual worker must perform to produce the means of her own livelihood. This surplus labor generates the "surplus value" that constitutes the capitalist's profit. While the proletarian's contribution is excessive, consisting of more than she can afford to spare, the capitalist can enrich himself excessively because he controls the means of production and is thereby able to press the dispossessed worker into service for a fraction of what her labor is really worth.

---

1 Karl Marx, *Capital*, vol. 1, trans. Ben Fowkes (New York: Penguin, 1976), 782.

Those who constitute the redundant population, this social waste, are often treated as though they are morally culpable for their position, even though their unemployment is structurally integral to capitalism — they are the strikebreakers-in-waiting ensuring that employers can keep wages low. We even criminalize unemployment with anti-loafing and vagrancy statutes and by making gainful employment a condition of probation and parole, the violation of which may result in incarceration. Social failings and structural inequities are transformed into personal failings by that piece of capitalist legerdemain Margaret Thatcher availed herself of when she famously declared that "there is no such thing as society. There are individual men and women."[2] This exaggerated theory of the individual holds that we move through the world, each one of us, neither aided nor encumbered by attachments or external barriers. Saying we are free cannot set us free. This description erases human finitude and blames the victim.

In a world in which finitude has been erased from discourse, not only are all limitations presumed to lie within the individual, all limitations are also presumed to be removable, surmountable by those who are sufficiently strong-willed. The interrelatedness of all things is forgotten. "Being an individual *de jure*," Zygmunt Bauman writes, "means having no one to blame for one's own misery, seeking the causes of one's own defeats nowhere except in one's own indolence and sloth, and looking for no remedies other than trying harder and harder still."[3] This is the "performance principle," which Herbert Marcuse understands as a self-administered authoritarian regime in disguise, the ethos of "an acquisitive and antagonistic society in the process of constant expansion," in which "domination has been increasingly rationalized."[4] In such societies, the perfor-

2 Margaret Thatcher, "AIDS, Education and the Year 2000!" interview by Douglas Keay, *Woman's Own* (October 31, 1987).
3 Zygmunt Bauman, *Wasted Lives: Modernity and Its Outcasts* (New York: Phaidon Press, 1964), 38.
4 Herbert Marcuse, *Eros and Civilization: A Philosophical Inquiry into Freud* (Boston: Beacon Press, 1955), 45.

mance principle displaces the pleasure principle, work replacing enjoyment. While workers today may in general have more of an ability to choose the type of work they do, "their labor is work for an apparatus which they do not control, which operates as an independent power to which individuals must submit if they want to live."[5] The foreman who presided over Marx's nineteenth-century factories, policing efficiency and facilitating the extraction of labor from the worker to enrich the capitalist, may no longer be ubiquitous, but only because the foreman is no longer necessary, Marcuse argues. Jon McKenzie asserts that the performance principle is something we come to internalize, rendering that which cannot be "rationalized" useless or excessive, wasteful. "The performance principle entails the repressive sublimation of human desire," as desire is chaotic and supremely inefficient when left unattended.[6] Capitalism harnesses desire, reterritorializes it.

Dramaturgies of Waste

On Western stages, the dominant dramaturgy of the nineteenth century was a dramaturgy of efficiency, the so-called "well-made play," as developed by the French playwright Eugène Scribe and subsequently imitated widely in Europe and the United States. The well-made play was formulaic, with intricate, technically well-executed exchanges of plot-propelling information taking precedence over nuanced character development or ideas. The well-made play used and reused generic stories and situations in order to reliably provoke an emotional response in audiences. As Wilkie Collins summed up the formula: "Make 'em laugh; make 'em weep; make 'em wait." In the well-made play, there is nothing excessive; the buildup of suspense is crucial, but all loose ends get tied up by the time the curtain falls. As one admirer of the form puts it, "Each scene must make a defi-

---

5   Ibid.
6   Jon McKenzie, *Perform or Else: From Discipline to Performance* (New York: Routledge, 2001), 160.

nite contribution to the development of the action. [...] [T]he combination of characters to be found onstage at a given moment is determined mainly by the potential for the transfer of information."[7] The well-made play invites the spectator to admire the choreography of bodies and operative language; the spectacle is exquisitely self-contained: "the primary and most consistent characteristic of the well-made play is the thoroughness with which every action, every event, even every entrance and exit is prepared, explained, justified."[8]

The twentieth century, however, saw the rise of playwrights who sought to reclaim a space for inefficiency and excess in the theater. As nonproductive expenditure becomes increasingly circumscribed in our late-capitalist lives, we increasingly see artists turning to it as an aesthetic strategy in their work. These dramaturgies of waste, as I call them, have both formal and ideological dimensions. Like modernism itself, dramaturgies of waste are characterized by the questioning and rejection of received forms. Early examples include playwrights concerned with critically re-inhabiting traditional models of dramatic structure. By the century's end, however, we see playwrights invested in emptying or canceling out structure itself, a reclamation of nonproductive expenditure and an act of resistance against the capitalist regimes of efficiency that organize our lives outside the theater. Today, dramaturgies of waste have embraced negativity to such a degree that formlessness may become the twenty-first century's legacy.

Failures of Sublimation: Harley Granville-Barker

English playwright Harley Granville-Barker cut his teeth as an actor in the plays of his near-contemporary George Bernard Shaw, and the two shared a proprietary stake in what is sometimes called the "drama of ideas." What distinguished these plays

---

7   Douglas Cardwell, "The Well-Made Play of Eugène Scribe," *The French Review* 56, no. 6 (1983): 879.
8   Ibid., 882.

from their nineteenth-century forebears was that they were *about* something, some more-or-less pressing social or political issue of the day. In a drama of ideas, an extended disquisition on theories of progress or empire put into the mouth of a character is not a detour from or interruption of the unfolding of the plot — it is itself the substance of the drama. The plot is largely relegated to being the delivery system for that content. Characters stand for particular points of view, hypotheses about the way the world is or should be, and their actions and outcomes function as tests of those hypotheses. Today, plays that proceed by developing a complex theme are commonplace, but at the turn of the twentieth century, such a deviation from the "well-made" model represented what can be seen as a subtle shift away from the prevailing valorization of efficiency in storytelling and toward a dramaturgy of waste. Such plays offered opportunities for provocation, contemplation, and reconsideration. The drama of ideas introduced a mode of engaging with the theatrical event that defied the performance principle, calling for a slower speed, a more attentive ear, and potentially for an unsettling of settled worldviews.

In his 1907 play *Waste*, Granville-Barker takes up the *agōn* between unsublimated desire and the performance principle, eros and civilization, rendering it as a gendered opposition. In the Victorian era, which drew to a close shortly before the play's composition, gender roles became sharply defined, with the public sphere largely reserved for men and the domestic sphere left to women.[9] People also responded to the dramatic transformation of social and economic life brought about by industrialization with concern about child labor and the welfare of working families. In an increasingly hard-edged, dirty, dense, urban landscape, women were tasked with cultivating a soft, private, refined space where the bodies and souls of children and men could be nourished and recreated. The distinction between men as producers and women as reproducers took a firm hold. While

---

9 Margaret Hewitt, *Wives and Mothers in Victorian Industry* (London: Rockliff, 1958), 153–54.

the complementary importance of both spheres would not generally have been in question, every binary becomes a hierarchy. As Hélène Cixous observes, we have:

> Activity/passivity...
> Culture/Nature...
> Intelligible/Palpable...
> Form, convex, step, advance, semen, progress.
> Matter, concave, ground — where steps are taken, holding- and dumping-ground.
> <u>Man</u>
> Woman[10]

Since "thought has always worked through opposition," if the public sphere was where men confidently made use of their "higher" faculties, the domestic sphere, we are left to assume, was where women groped around in the dark with only their "lower" faculties to guide them.[11] Generally incapable of sublimation, as Freud put it, "woman finds herself forced into the background by the claims of civilization and she adopts a hostile attitude towards it."[12] Woman becomes the dumping ground of culture. Patriarchy translates her negativity away as hostility.

Waste basically accepts the Freudian paradigm; it is a play that loathes women. More interesting for its blind spots and omissions than for its declarative statements, *Waste* follows ambitious politician Henry Trebell as his life unravels in the wake of a scandal instigated by a failure of sublimation. Trebell is an important man, a politician, an ostensibly progressive man. For much of the play, he is busy working on a bill to disestablish the Church of England. He is a hard-bitten materialist who consid-

---

10 Hélène Cixous and Catherine Clément, "Sorties: Out and Out: Attacks/Ways Out/Forays," in *The Newly Born Woman*, trans. Betsy Wing (London: I.B. Tauris, 1996), 63.
11 Ibid.
12 Sigmund Freud, "Civilization and Its Discontents," in *The Freud Reader*, ed. Peter Gay, trans. James Strachey (London: W.W. Norton & Company, 1989), 745.

ers love to be "a waste of time."[13] Summarizing his perspective on passion, Trebell declares that "[t]here are three facts in life that call up emotion . . Birth, Death, and the Desire for Children. The niceties are shams."[14] His behavior toward women is consistent with this philosophy. When the married Amy O'Connell confesses to him that their clandestine tryst some months ago resulted in a pregnancy that cannot be attributed to her husband who has been in another country for over a year, she is frightened, despairing, indignant that by accident of biology she must bear this shame alone. "Oh, the physical curse of being a woman," she rails, "no better than any savage in this condition . . worse off than an animal. It's unfair."[15] She asks Trebell if the evening they spent together meant anything to him, and he replies, "[l]isten. I look back on that night as one looks back on a fit of drunkenness."[16] She confirms, "[y]ou mean I might have been any other woman," and he replies, apparently ingenuously, "[w]ouldn't any other woman have served the purpose[?]"[17]

Amy's enforced passivity proves intolerable. "You don't know what it is to have a thing happening in spite of you," she complains to her unmoved, erstwhile lover.[18] Wounded by his indifference and unable to countenance bearing the child of a man who does not love her, Amy seeks out a doctor willing to perform a back-alley abortion. The dangerous procedure results in her death. When the scandal outs and Trebell's colleagues learn that he is responsible for the whole sordid affair, they decide they can no longer work with him. He is ousted from their coalition, his life's work destroyed. For confused reasons, partly an inability to see the purpose of life now that his career is over, partly a desire to make his colleagues rue the day they cast him

---

13 Harley Granville-Barker, *Waste*, in *Three Plays: The Marrying off Ann Leete, The Voysey Inheritance, Waste* (London: Sidgwick & Jackson, 1909), 235.
14 Ibid., 236.
15 Ibid., 257–58.
16 Ibid., 258.
17 Ibid., 259.
18 Ibid., 255.

out, Trebell kills himself. In the final line of the play, Trebell's secretary bemoans the suicide: "I'm angry . . just angry at the waste of a good man. Look at the work undone . . think of it! Who is to do it! Oh . . the waste . . !"[19]

We are invited to recognize Trebell's death as the "waste" of the play's title, to see his death as a tragedy, the great but flawed man unjustly felled by a single foolish mistake. Amy O'Connell's death goes largely unmourned. As recently as 2000, the critic John Simon dismissed the character of Amy O'Connell as "highly neurotic."[20] If neuroses are symptomatic of an imperfect ability or unwillingness to adjust to the demands of culture, she is a neurotic simply by virtue of her gender. The play pits the "masculine" virtues of detachment, order, and discipline against the destructively "feminine" vices of attachment, chaos, and desire. Diametrically opposed and irreconcilable, "there's no such thing as a sexual relationship."[21] In private life, such as it is, and in work, *efficiency*, Trebell remarks on more than one occasion, should be of paramount consideration. The rest is a waste of time.

If *Waste* is about a life destroyed by a failure of sublimation, a fatal hiccup in a life otherwise strictly ordered in accordance with the performance principle, Granville-Barker's 1905 *The Voysey Inheritance* is about a surfeit of sublimation and the ruin it brings to a family. The Voysey patriarch, like his father before him, is a financier. His firm has a reputation for expeditiously making money into more money. As heir apparent to the firm, Edward Voysey learns, however, that his father and grandfather have long been helping themselves to the funds other people have entrusted to them, speculating with their clients' capital, "pocketing the gains, cutting the losses; meanwhile paying the

---

19 Ibid., 342.
20 John Simon, "Waste," *New York Magazine,* March 27, 2000, https://nymag.com/nymetro/arts/theater/reviews/2487/.
21 Jacques Lacan, *On Feminine Sexuality: The Limits of Love and Knowledge,* trans. Bruce Fink (New York: Norton, 1998), 12.

client his ordinary income."[22] By the time Edward is old enough to hear the truth, the firm is deeply compromised. The family's homes, their fine clothes, Edward's sister's dowry — all of it has been purchased with stolen money and the elder Mr. Voysey is in much too deep to be able to pay it back even if he wanted to.

He does at least claim to want to set things right. Mr. Voysey's story is that he inherited this sorry state of affairs from his own father and has righteously dedicated his life to wrangling the debt down to a manageable size. Edwards later discovers that this is a lie, that his father did at one point manage to get the firm in the clear, only to begin illicitly speculating again fifteen years later. But Mr. Voysey has every intention, he tells his son, of catching up before the time has come for Edward to take the helm of the firm. Edward protests that if his father had really wanted to make amends, he would have "lived poor" and devoted himself to his client's good and not to his own aggrandizement.[23] But Mr. Voysey does not see it that way: "[w]hat has carried me to victory," he asks his son, but "the confidence of my clients. What has earned that confidence? A decent life, my integrity, my brains? No, my reputation for wealth . . that, and nothing else. Business now-a-days is run on the lines of the confidence trick."[24] Without giving his clientele the impression that he was enjoying considerable success, Voysey argues, he would never have been able to convince them to keep investing. Without their investments, he would never be able to turn a profit, and the whole corrupt edifice would come crashing down. Voysey is not wrong. Capitalism itself *is* a kind of Ponzi scheme, depending on ever-increasing populations, resources, and levels of consumption in order to sustain itself. A cosmic confidence trick is all that keeps it going. There may be no such thing as a financier who is both successful and scrupulously honest.

---

22 Harley Granville-Barker, *The Voysey Inheritance* (Boston: Little, Brown, and Company, 1916), 67.
23 Ibid., 45.
24 Ibid., 46.

Edward takes a youthfully idealistic hard line against this justification, only to find himself tempted by it after his father's untimely demise. To confess everything would mean not only hurting his own family, who have, after all, become accustomed to a certain style of living, but further hurting his clients as well. Once the truth comes out, there will be no chance of Edward's recovering even the principal for anyone, but as long as no one knows the game he is playing, he can still hold out hope of catching up. He soon finds himself taking up the family business. The only adjustment he makes is that he reprioritizes recuperating the investments of his less well-to-do clients over those of his wealthier clients.

Women prove pivotal in *The Voysey Inheritance*. In *Waste*, Amy O'Connell stood for the hero's tragic flaw, embodying all the stereotypical shortcomings of femininity, but the women of *The Voysey Inheritance* exist on a spectrum of worthlessness. At the end of *Waste*, while everyone else is lamenting the death of the great man, a pair of female characters spare a moment to reflect on what became of Amy. "When will men learn to know one woman from another," one asks.[25] Her companion replies, "[w]hen will all women care to be one thing rather than the other?"[26] The supposed indistinguishability of women is attributed not to any deficiency of male vision or attention but to some pernicious female conspiracy. By contrast, in *The Voysey Inheritance*, several models of femininity are proposed. Edward's sister Honor is introduced by a striking, gratuitously cruel stage direction indicating that the world would be better off if she were dead. "Poor Honor," as she is called, "is a phenomenon common to most large families. From her earliest years she has been bottle washer to her brothers. While they were expensively educated, she was grudged schooling; her highest accomplishment was meant to be mending their clothes."[27] The playwright goes on to tell us of Honor's parents' general distaste for her sex,

---

25 Granville-Barker, *Waste*, 340.
26 Ibid.
27 Granville-Barker, *The Voysey Inheritance*, 30.

then continues, "[i]n a less humane society she would have been exposed at birth."[28] Honor is barely tolerated, and her existence assumed meaningless, presumably because she has never had any marriage prospects and spends her time scurrying around fetching cigars for the men in her family. One of her brothers wonders aloud, "I wonder they bothered to give her a name."[29] Honor is not an important character in the sense of driving the action of the play forward in a significant way. Granville-Barker seems to include her merely to demonstrate that there is such a thing as a woman who is less valuable even than a dumping ground.

The other women are the products of their economic status, determined by their access to capital down to the way they experience desire. Beatrice, married to one of the Voysey brothers is asked if she married for love. She replies: "I've had to earn my own living, consequently there isn't one thing in my life that I have ever done quite genuinely for its own sake . . but always with an eye toward bread-and-butter, pandering to the people who were to give me that."[30] Juxtaposed with her is Alice, Edward's paramour, who is independently wealthy and therefore equipped to selflessly redeem Edward when he is at last found out. They will be married, she assures him, and her income will suffice to sustain them. Their only problem is that, should he go to prison, she will have to be careful not to be excessively proud of him. "My heart praises you," she tells him just before the final curtain comes down.[31] Perhaps she is proud of him for facing the music, though if he could avoid doing so, it seems he surely would. Perhaps she perversely feels as though there is something chic about having a spouse who has done time for white-collar crime.

Alice (and her money) undo the emergent morals of *The Voysey Inheritance*. It turns out that crime does pay. Woman, with

---

28 Ibid.
29 Ibid., 116.
30 Ibid., 38.
31 Ibid., 130.

her less robustly-developed superego can always be counted upon to enable, forgive, and recompense. The Voyseys oversublimated, forgetting that the figures in their ledgers meant something tangible to actual people. Alice undersublimates, taking it upon herself to break Edward's fall with sexual absolution. Here, rather than complement one another, eros and civilization bring out the worst in each other.

Ibsen: "Life Is Work"

Henrik Ibsen elaborated on — some say perfected — Scribe's well-made play, elevating the form into something substantial enough to bear the weight of such complex themes as the problem of the individual in relationship to society. Ibsen also made ample use of the nineteenth century's other major popular theatrical genre, melodrama. Where the well-made play privileged technique and intrigue, the melodrama's emphasis was on emotion. In the classic *mélodrames* of August von Kotzebue and Guilbert de Pixérécourt, the dramatic action was accompanied by continuous musical underscoring, which guided and heightened the audience's emotional experience. Also exaggerated in melodrama are the stakes of the conflicts driving the plot. On the surface, melodramas appear to be about a family that can't pay the rent or the virgin ingenue's seduction by the corrupt aristocrat. The melodramatic imagination, however, is Manichaean, that is, perceiving the world as divided along the lines of absolute good and absolute evil. At its most primal, melodrama is just this naked conflict. As Eric Bentley argues, melodrama "is drama in its elemental form; it is the quintessence of drama."[32] Melodrama is emotionally excessive, because it exceeds itself — the laughter of the moustache-twirling villain is not the villain's alone but satanic laughter.

In the nineteenth century, melodrama was also typically marked by the godlike intercession of "poetic justice," which unfailingly ensured that the virtuous prosper while the ne'er-

---

32 Eric Bentley, *The Life of the Drama* (New York: Athenuem, 1964), 202.

do-wells got their comeuppance. As the genre congealed, it too became formulaic, working to reinforce conventional conservative values by punishing the wicked outsiders and libertines by the time the curtain fell, while sparing the righteously chaste defenders of honor, home, and country. One of Ibsen's contributions to modern drama was the way in which he often used melodrama as a kind of red herring, adopting many of the trappings of the form only to subvert the genre's clearly defined polarities. Rather than presenting clearly delineated, internally consistent representatives of good and evil, Ibsen tends to make it difficult for his audiences to discern with any certainty who is doing the right thing for the right motives, the wrong thing for the wrong motives, or some combination of the two. There are neither true heroes nor villains in Ibsen, only human beings susceptible to venality and self-delusion, people struggling mightily with the various uncertainties introduced by the onset of modernity, people who more often than not do rash and regrettable things to escape the discomfort of such uncertainties.

Like the Voysey men, the eponymous protagonist of Ibsen's 1896 *John Gabriel Borkman* is a man whose outsize ambition and self-regard blind him to his own needs and the needs of those closest to him. Borkman is another financier who illegally speculated with his clients' money in an attempt to enrich himself. Once Borkman was caught, he lost everything and went to prison. The play begins eight years after he is released, but Borkman is still a prisoner, living separately from his unforgiving wife in their own home, never showing his face in public. He spends his days pacing the floor of the attic to which he has exiled himself. Like so many in his line of work, Borkman does not see himself as a thief; he is a zealous believer in the capitalist fantasy of infinite economic expansion. He maintains that with their money in his capable hands, his entire stable of unwitting investors would eventually have had their down payments on his future returned to them; Borkman planned to use the capital to fund a large-scale project extracting valuable minerals from the earth. But Borkman's motivations are complex. He is not exclusively inspired by cold self-interest. He legitimately believes that if he were to once again assume control of the appropriate resources, he would have "the power to create human happiness for vast multitudes around me."[33] The son of a miner, he comes from humble origins and is not indifferent to the struggles of the working class. Even so, Borkman's hubris eclipses in his mind the ethical implications of gambling with other people's money, and it ultimately leads to tragedy.

In his isolation, Borkman's embrace of capitalism takes on a perversely religious dimension. He equates the accumulation of wealth with the attainment of "the kingdom — and the power — and the glory," a quotation from the Gospel according to Matthew.[34] In the biblical scene from which the phrase is drawn, Christ is instructing his disciples in the proper way to pray. Addressing himself to the Father, Christ avows, "[f]or *thine* is the kingdom, the power, and the glory for ever."[35] The irony of Borkman's misappropriation of the locution is twofold if considered in the context of the Catholic Mass, during which worshipers still recite this doxology in response to the Lord's Prayer. At this moment during the liturgy, the entire congregation has taken hands, symbolically joining together as one body. All hands are then lifted heavenward together, signifying a community of believers united in self-abnegation. Borkman's sacrilegious rewrite both deposes God in favor of Mammon and erases all suggestion of a communitarian ethos.

What we call "futures trading" is big business on Wall Street today. This investment practice might well have appealed to both Borkman and his wife. Gunhild Borkman's obsession with attaining a personalized "kingdom" is as keen as her husband's. Being a nineteenth-century wife and mother, however, her path to power and glory differs. Now that living vicariously through her disgraced husband is no longer an option, she has invested all her hopes in her son Erhart. The language of finance

---

33 Henrik Ibsen, *John Gabriel Borkman*, in *Four Major Plays*, trans. Rolf Fjelde (New York: Penguin Books, 1970), 2:370.
34 Ibid., 394.
35 Matthew 6:13.

is ubiquitous in the play even and especially when characters are speaking of matters of the heart, but Gunhild's vocabulary is more religious than economic. Erhart, for example, presents Gunhild with a path to "restitution" for her wasted life.[36] Her son will undertake the "sacred mission" of restoring the honor of the family. By dedicating his life to an as-yet-to-be-determined noble cause — but certainly something substantive, legal, and dignified — he is expected to turn a profit for his mother in some cosmic sense, repaying the debt she is owed by his father.

Gunhild's mercenary model of motherhood is contrasted with that of her twin sister Ella Rentheim, who fostered Erhart when he was a child during the worst of the fraud scandal surrounding his father. Ella listens to her sister's grand plans for Erhart's future with alarm. Ella's maternal concern manifests in what appears to be a less self-serving way; she just wants to love and be loved by Erhart and to see him happy, like (as we later learn) she just wanted to love and be loved by his father many years ago. Gunhild's ideas about love are bound up with profit and possession. She adapts the avarice that drives her husband in the public sphere for use in the private sphere. Ella's attitude toward the young man's dalliance with a slightly older local woman is blasé, romance and pleasure-seeking being the prerogative of the young, in her view. Gunhild, by contrast, is deeply threatened. Not only is Erhart frittering away his valuable time at dances and the like, he is also drifting into another woman's sphere of influence, a woman young enough to be sexually appealing but mature enough to lead him from the straight and narrow path Gunhild has prescribed for him.

Before long, Ella reveals that she is not prepared to divest herself of her adopted son either. When she arrives at the Borkman's home, it is to stake her claim not to power over Erhart but to his name. If he disavows the name Borkman and agrees to carry on the name Rentheim, then they will forever be bound together as mother and son, a bond Ella covets more than ever now that her health is failing fast. Greed has devastated the lives

36 Ibid., 316.

of Borkman, Gunhild, and Ella, but Ella's is perhaps the most barren. Formerly in love with Borkman, she was rejected in favor of her sister because someone with the power to offer Borkman a promotion at the bank had fallen for Ella. Confronting Borkman, she says, "It's ages since the two of us met [...]. A whole lifetime between. A lifetime wasted [...]. For us both."[37] Borkman "abandoned [Ella] for higher incentives."[38]

> BORKMAN: I couldn't get on without his help. And he set you as his price.
> ELLA: And you paid the price. In full. Without a murmur.
> BORKMAN: I had no choice. It was win or go under.
> ELLA: (*her voice trembling, as she looks at him*). Is it really true what you say — that I was dearest in the world to you then?
> BORKMAN: Both then and after — long, long after.
> ELLA: And still you traded me away. Bargained your rightful love to another man. Sold my love for a — for a bank presidency.[39]

Borkman objects to Ella's assessment of their "wasted" lives. Perhaps she wasted hers. She could, after all, have married the man who came between the two of them. And Borkman made certain that while his own family and clients' fortunes disintegrated, she at least came out financially secure. But Ella and Borkman have no common vocabulary with which to productively discuss things like waste and necessity. "There's no such thing as a sexual relationship."[40] As Borkman explains:

> BORKMAN: I suppose it's very natural for you to see this the way you do. You're a woman. And so it seems, to your mind, that nothing else in the world exists or matters.

---

37 Ibid., 352.
38 Ibid., 355.
39 Ibid., 355–56.
40 Lacan, *On Feminine Sexuality*, 12.

ELLA: Yes, nothing else.
BORKMAN: Only what touches your own heart.
ELLA: Only that! Only that! Yes.
BORKMAN: But you have to remember that I'm a man. As a woman, to me, you were the dearest in the world. But in the last analysis, any woman can be replaced by another.[41]

Ella's doppelgänger Gunhild ends up with the man, who doesn't matter to her without the money, and Ella ends up with the money, which doesn't matter to her without the man. As women, they are interchangeable and expendable. "Oh, these women!" Borkman laments, "[t]hey corrupt and distort our lives! They completely botch up our destinies — our paths to glory."[42] Women distract, ensnare, draw men into a relational existence rather than allowing them to merely preside over their own lives and the lives of others. "Life is work," Borkman tells his son, hoping to save him from the dangerous pull of the feminine.[43] A familiar figure from Ibsen's oeuvre, Borkman is an "all or nothing" extremist. There can be no happy marriage of work and love, masculine and feminine. So he remains isolated, his emotional life as much of a wasteland as those of the two women who loved him. As Borkman finds himself nearing death, he stands alone with Ella in a small clearing high in the woods. Just at the moment when it seems he might repent, see the error of his ways, tell his beloved that he was wrong to forsake her, Borkman instead delivers a melancholy ode to the untapped potential of his true love — rocks:

BORKMAN: I can sense them, the buried millions. I feel the veins of metal reaching their curving, branching, beckoning arms out to me. I saw them before me like living shadows — the night I stood in the bank vault with a lantern in my hand. You wanted your freedom then — and I tried to

---

41 Ibid., 357.
42 Ibid., 348.
43 Ibid., 376.

> set you free. But I lacked the strength for it. Your treasures sank back into the depths.[44]

So, too, have Ella's treasures sunk back into the depths. Left uncultivated, her body and soul are wasted, landscapes rich in resources never harvested, never put to any use. But Ella was never looking for a return on her investment, as Gunhild was; Ella wanted to spend herself but found the market closed. In *Borkman,* Ibsen shows how when love and work are at odds, the harder of the two to quantify is often the loser. Only one currency is accepted here; the rest is waste.

Policing Catharsis: The Passion of Politics and the Politics of Passion in Brecht

Bertolt Brecht's expressly anti-capitalist epic theater was highly waste-conscious, but Brecht's was the obverse of a dramaturgy of waste. Brecht instead resisted the performance principle by attempting to carefully regulate the economy of emotion in the theater. Rather than letting inflamed passions overflow or run to extremes as in melodrama, Brecht believed that catharsis was too precious a thing to waste on an aesthetic experience. Catharsis should rather be instrumentalized, put in service of altering the material abjection of the human condition. According to Brecht's liberationist worldview, the basic facts of social reality are subject to change. Because the present conditions of social existence are always already the result of specific human actions, specific human actions can be undertaken today to willfully shape the conditions of social existence tomorrow.

Brecht defined his epic theater as the antithesis of Aristotelian tragedy, which he saw as politically enervating. The experience of catharsis purges the spectator of pity and fear, but for Brecht this purgation represented a waste of emotions that could and ought to be put to better use. Properly incited and channeled, pity and fear could be fomented into righteous rage that could propel the spectator from her seat into the street to

---

44 Ibid., 394.

join the revolution. Tragedy, Brecht thought, left the spectator drained, resigned to her fate, and prepared to tolerate even what ought to be intolerable. Brecht's dramaturgy was shaped by the anti-fatalistic belief that the body in pain could be liberated by the mind, by *homo faber,* architect of better futures and other possible worlds. Brecht sought to appeal to the spectator's intellect — emotion should remain bottled up as fuel for struggles to come. During his lifetime, Brecht objected when his plays were performed in an overly emotional style, in a style that invited catharsis, as though each drop of incidentally spilled sentiment reduced the potency of his larger project.

The irrepressibly pathos-inducing *Mother Courage and Her Children,* co-authored with Margarete Steffin, gave Brecht more than its fair share of trouble in this respect. Leopold Lindtberg helmed the 1941 premiere production, and audiences were overcome by the sympathy they felt for the heroine, Anna Fierling, who loses her children one by one while roaming Europe during the Thirty Years' War (1618–1648), staying alive by selling provisions to soldiers of any affiliation out of a cart she drags behind her. Brecht thought that this empathic response demonstrated an inadequate exercise of the *Verfremdungseffekt,* or alienation effect, on the part of the actors and an inadequate understanding of it on the part of the spectators. The ideal, Brechtian actor was to stand some distance apart from and comment on rather than *be* the character. Brecht frequently used humor and cultivated incongruity to interrupt the flow of narrative and interfere with emotional momentum. Suspense was to be avoided by telegraphing the events of the plot using text displayed on placards so that audiences could focus not so much on what happened as on how and why it was happening. Though Brecht tried to make it more difficult for audiences to sympathize with Anna Fierling, the how and why of *Mother Courage* — brutal economic necessity — has often been subsumed by the what — the death of the innocent. At the climax of the play, Fierling has only one child remaining, the mute Katrin. Katrin climbs up to a rooftop, begins beating a drum to warn the villagers of approaching soldiers, and is shot dead. Historically, it has proven nearly impossible to stage the play's climax without calling forth an emotional response.

The affective potential of the play, however, need not be seen as a pitfall to be avoided. In *The Death of Tragedy,* George Steiner observes that Brecht, though he would have denied it, gave us a new kind of tragedy, the "tragedy of waste." In this context, waste means loss, senseless destruction, meaningless suffering — the waste of the capitalist system that in Brecht's plays appears in human terms. Where Aristotelian tragedy generates pity and fear by emphasizing human helplessness — the inevitability of our ultimately succumbing to forces more powerful than ourselves — a tragedy of waste such as *Mother Courage* presents suffering that is terrible to behold precisely because it is *not* inevitable. In a tragedy of waste, the events that produce the suffering are presented as avoidable, the results of human choices rather than divine mandate or natural law. According to Steiner, *Mother Courage* is an allegory of pure waste not only because the heroine loses all of her children, but because she learns nothing from her experience.[45] There is no scene of recognition, no lamentation. The play closes with Fierling leaving her daughter's body for some peasant women to bury, taking up her wagon again, and trundling off down the road to continue following the soldiers, her market, intoning, "I must get back to business."[46]

The "tragedy of waste" is what Steiner proposed as a possible survivor of what he identified as the "death of tragedy" proper in the Western dramatic tradition. With the West having lost its grasp on religious faith, Steiner argued, our culture no longer possesses in common an adequate shared background for tragedy, a shared set of myths or creeds concerning how human destiny is arbitrated by higher forces. Raymond Williams responds to Steiner by arguing that even if the pagan pantheons

---

45 George Steiner, *The Death of Tragedy* (New Haven: Yale University Press, 1996), 346.
46 Bertolt Brecht, *Mother Courage and Her Children,* trans. Eric Bentley (New York: Grove Press, 1955), 111.

are in ruins and God is dead, Western peoples still share plenty of beliefs — the belief in the invincibility of global capitalism is among the most powerful. One need not be a church-going Protestant to endorse and strive to live by a Protestant work ethic, eschewing idleness and devoting oneself to enhancing one's performance, increasing one's productivity.

Though it is not set during wartime, Brecht's 1943 *The Good Person of Setzuan* demonstrates that capitalist "peace" retains much of the violence that characterizes periods of official conflict. *Good Person* is a tragedy of waste in which the heroine learns something and is literally transformed by the acquisition of knowledge. Brecht originally intended to title the play *Die Ware Liebe* (*The Product Love*), reflecting his conviction that even love, affection, and altruism can be commodified, reterritorialized by capitalism. The heroine of *Good Person* is Shen Teh, a virtuous young prostitute. The gods come to visit Shen Teh's province and find that she alone has not forsaken their principles. Poor as she is, Shen Teh is generous and charitable, while greed has consumed the rest of her community. The gods give Shen Teh a sum of money in exchange for the hospitality she shows them and also to see if her virtue will hold up once she knows how it feels to have something to lose. Shen Teh buys a tobacco shop and soon finds that the more she has, the more her neighbors need from her. To avoid being ruinously exploited while struggling to manage their demands, Shen Teh assumes the identity of her fictional cousin, the hardheaded and unyielding Shui Ta, a male authority figure who has no difficulty saying no to those in need. She learns that capitalism loves only the lonely. Feminine selflessness and passionate attachment are liabilities Shen Teh must forsake in favor of Shui Ta's masculine individualism if she is to survive. Though she has never been more affluent, for the first time, she is truly afraid.

A perennial problem with the scarcity mentality inculcated by an economics of fear is that it creates inequality from abundance. A society built on fear becomes a society of anxiety once fear has fulfilled its function, when stability and broadly shared prosperity is within reach. Anxiety has no purpose or object, but it cannot be reasoned away. It lingers, telling us that we are not safe, that we are not enough, don't have enough, that the catastrophe is right around the corner. In *Good Person,* that anxiety leads to the exploited becoming the exploiter. While Shui Ta is called into being to eliminate waste, he takes to his role so well that he becomes the "Tobacco King of Setzuan," owner of an ever-expanding business and a factory that employs more than twice the lawful number of workers. Shen Teh falls in love with a depressed, unemployed pilot only to have him use her for money, get her pregnant, and abandon her. As her pregnancy progresses, Shen Teh struggles to conceal her femininity, even as the business she runs as Shui Ta becomes a more and more high-stakes enterprise, the pressure to perform as a hypermasculine taskmaster ramping ever-upwards. The transformation prompted by Shen Teh's acquisition of knowledge alienates her from herself and ultimately leaves her crying out in vain for help to the sympathetic, but useless, gods. The play's epilogue situates the possibility for truly revolutionary transformation in the audience, asking, "[c]an the world be changed? […] You write the happy ending to the play! There must, there must, there's got to be a way!"[47] Deliberately denying the audience catharsis, Brecht seeks to catalyze political action with aesthetic frustration.

Postdramatic Theater/Postideological Theater

Brechtian dramaturgy exposes the means of production to prevent dramatic absorption, to train the spectator to regard the world outside the theater skeptically, and to furnish the spectator with the basic tools of Marxist analysis. A more recent revolution in Western theatrical form creates even more distance between theater and drama. Brechtian theater invites the spectator to take a close and critical look at cause and effect, while what Hans-Thies Lehmann has termed "postdramatic theater" declines to treat narrative causation as the primary fulcrum

---

47 Bertolt Brecht, *The Good Woman of Setzuan,* trans. Eric Bentley (New York: Grove Press, 1956), 141.

of the theatrical event at all. Postdramatic theater largely does away with the "fictive cosmos" crucial to the coherence of much dramatic theater. Rather than inviting spectators to "suspend disbelief" and temporarily invest in the independent reality of the world of the play behind the proscenium arch, postdramatic theater acknowledges that the theatrical event is taking place in time and space shared by performer and spectator, permitting rupture and irruptions of the real. Yet, for Lehmann, postdramatic theater is not a theater that exists "'beyond' drama, without any relation to it."[48] Postdramatic theater still measures its distance from drama. It is still mourning and recovering from drama. According to Lehmann, postdramatic theater should be understood as "the unfolding and blossoming of a potential of disintegration, dismantling, and deconstruction within drama itself."[49]

While not a unified style or movement, the work characterized by Lehmann as postdramatic shares a few general formal features. In addition to the elimination of the intact fictive cosmos, postdramatic theater de-hierarchizes the various theatrical elements that have traditionally been organized in service of the text. Borrowing a grammatical term, Lehmann calls this new ordering of things "parataxis." Light, sound, costume, rhythm, and spatiality are no longer subordinated to a text as in the dramatic theater; they are not subordinated to anything at all, but rather *coordinated*. There is no default center, no spine. New combinations of intelligences inform the composers of postdramatic theatrical scores.

According to Aristotle, the ideal drama should have a certain magnitude. A vanishingly brief drama, like an infinitesimally small creature in nature, lacks the duration or dimension to be properly beheld. On the other hand, a drama that is too long and sprawling cannot be embraced by the mind of the spectator; the unity of the whole escapes us. "Beauty," Aristotle tells us,

---

48 Hans-Thies Lehmann, *Postdramatic Theatre*, trans. Karen Jürs-Munby (New York: Routledge, 2006), 44.
49 Ibid.

WASTE

"is a matter of size and order."[50] Postdramatic theater strives for something other than that which Aristotle, advocate of moderation in all things, would have found beautiful. In postdramatic theater, "[t]here is either too much or too little."[51] Postdramatic theater tends to inundate and withhold, sometimes simultaneously. It runs to the extremes of form, "the wasteland of unseizable extension and labyrinthine chaotic accumulation."[52]

These approaches dispel passive, total absorption and demand a different type of engagement from spectators. In psychoanalysis, Lehmann tells us, the term "evenly hovering attention" is used to characterize the way the analyst listens to the analysand.[53] This is the kind of attention that postdramatic theater requires. The dramatic theater, particularly of the tidily packaged, Scribean variety, sought to delight, to ingratiate itself with the spectator. The dramatic theater was an efficient employee, but the postdramatic theater is a frequently uncooperative analysand, structurally selfish, needy, and often ultimately unknowable. An unusual amount of patience may be required with this patient. In the psychoanalytic context, "everything depends on not understanding immediately." Like the analyst's, the postdramatic spectator's perception must "remain open for connections, correspondences and clues at completely unexpected moments, perhaps casting what was said earlier in a completely new light."[54] Meaning is deferred, perhaps indefinitely.

In psychoanalysis, a session might be quiet and uneventful, with a recalcitrant patient offering only a cough here or a twitch there to give the analyst anything to go on. In another session, a patient might release a torrent of memories or tears or recriminations. Similarly, in the postdramatic theater, the density and intensity of signs may vary. The performance may try to seduce, disorient, repel, or remain aloof, but the spectator must do the

---

50 Aristotle, *On Poetry and Style,* trans. G.M.A. Grube (Indianapolis: Hackett Publishing Company, 1989), 16.
51 Lehmann, *Postdramatic Theatre,* 89.
52 Ibid., 90.
53 Ibid., 87.
54 Ibid.

work of determining what is of import. Postdramatic theater, like psychoanalysis and the psyche itself, is *inefficient*. It generates a great deal of apparent waste in the form of either excessive stimuli or empty, underutilized time and space. Of course, in the theater, nothing is really wasted. The theater's prodigiously wasteful economy of meaning can only be possible, and ethical, because time and space, the theater's basic ingredients, are infinitely renewable resources — our *only* infinitely renewable resources.

Wallace Shawn's Predramatic/Postdramatic Soliloquies

Wallace Shawn's monologue-driven plays present a paradox of classification; they can be understood as either pre-or postdramatic. Lehmann's precursor Peter Szondi saw postdramatic theater arising out of a crisis of the dialogic form, a crisis of confidence in the ability of the human subject to communicate its content in language. Lehmann noted that in postdramatic theater, monological and choral structures come to supersede dialogical structures. Shawn's *The Fever* exists in this postdramatic space while simultaneously harkening back to the earliest theatrical artifacts of Western civilization, notably *Prometheus Bound*. *The Fever*'s action, such as it is, is narrated, not dramatized. It toys, however, with eliminating the fictive cosmos, allowing Shawn to give voice to his own actual beliefs about his own actual class.

When Shawn first staged it in 1990, he chose to perform *The Fever* in private apartments rather than in a theater, and he chose to perform the sole role himself. He hoped to avoid making something that would be consumed as mere entertainment and to allow the theatrical event to be consumed by the real. Shawn has explained, "I'm trying to TELL somebody something that I MEAN. And you can't do that in a theater, because if you put a person on stage in a theater, that person will be interpreted as a character in a story."⁵⁵ *The Fever* has since been performed by other actors, but the sole speaker is unmistakably Shawn, scion of Manhattan literati, educated at Harvard and Oxford, connoisseur of the finer things in life. In *The Fever,* he reports that his hitherto pleasant, privileged life begins to putrefy after he reads Marx, which he does "at the very same time that Communism had finally died."⁵⁶ Referring to the fall of the Berlin Wall, which took place just a few months before the first performances of *The Fever,* Shawn also here invokes "The End of History," the essay in which Francis Fukuyama announced that the end of the Cold War presaged more than the end of a particular era of geopolitical conflict but of the end of history itself. "We may be witnessing," Fukuyama wrote, "the end point of mankind's ideological evolution and the universalization of Western liberal democracy as the final form of human government."⁵⁷ With the fall of the Soviet Union, Fukuyama believed, the Western liberal democratic model stands alone and vindicated because "the class issue has actually been successfully resolved in the West."⁵⁸

The Fever questions this conclusion. The play begins as an account of the scales falling from its speaker's eyes. A devoted lifelong student of his own thoughts and feelings — those things that make the speaker, he believes, an individual and an ethically solvent human being — the speaker has missed the obvious. More than his particular taste in classical music, relationships with intriguing friends and cherished family, or opinions about politics, it is his class that makes him who he is. It is his class that has made it possible for him to grow up believing that things like his taste and opinions are special or significant at all. Because, as Shawn has said, "America has a blind spot on the issue of money and class," in *The Fever,* everything but class falls

---

55 Wallace Shawn, "The Art of Theater No. 17," interviewed by Hilton Als, *The Paris Review* 201 (summer 2012), https://www.theparisreview.org/interviews/6154/wallace-shawn-the-art-of-theater-no-17-wallace-shawn.
56 Wallace Shawn, *The Fever* (New York: Grove Press, 1991), 19.
57 Francis Fukuyama, "The End of History?" *The National Interest* 16 (1989): 4.
58 Ibid., 9.

away. People are reduced to their class privilege, or lack thereof, and it becomes impossible to ignore the issue.

When the speaker of *The Fever* begins to become aware of the relationship between his pleasure and the pain of the poor both in his own city and in far-flung beleaguered nations convulsed by revolution, he becomes afflicted by constant, violent nausea. The play begins with the speaker lurching to the bathroom to kneel before the toilet. He has recently received, as an anonymous gift, a copy of Marx's *Capital*. Soon after, he visits a series of poor countries, where at first he cannot help romanticizing, aestheticizing them. He eats the ice cream that the wealthy people of the countries eat in glittering restaurants while the poor rebels are raped and tortured out of sight. One day, the ice cream he had been inhaling with such relish begins to taste bland and unappetizing. His enjoyment is gone. "I'd always said," the speaker reflects, "'I'm a happy person. I love life,' but now there was a sort of awful indifference or blankness that was coming from somewhere inside me and filling me up, bit by bit. Things that would once have delighted me or cheered me seemed to go dead on me, to spoil."[59] The depression persists.

As is often the case in Shawn's work, the body and the mind are not fully synchronized. The speaker is plagued by physical torments long before he is able to understand what is rotten on an intellectual or sociopolitical level. Over the course of the play, he confronts a chambermaid who sleeps in filth and Marxist revolutionaries imprisoned or murdered for their convictions, along with other human refuse of global capitalism. These encounters force the speaker to confront the fact that he is directly responsible for these people and has in fact *produced* them. His fate and the chambermaid's are linked. Her existence, the filth she sleeps in, her ignorance and poverty are the cost of his prosperity. He does not own the factories. He does not set wages or determine the length of the working day. But his habits of consumption alone render him culpable, "the end of history" notwithstanding. "[W]e can't escape our connection to the poor,"

---

59 Shawn, *The Fever*, 26.

the speaker says, because "[w]ithout the poor to get the fruit off the trees, to tend the excrement under the ground, to bathe our babies on the day they're born, we couldn't exist. Without the poor to do awful work, we would spend our lives doing awful work."[60] For Shawn, because capitalism has not liberated the chambermaid, capitalism has not been vindicated. *The Fever* poses a challenge to Fukuyama's post-ideological narrative of world history, suggesting that ideology is most insidious when invisible, when we allow ourselves to be persuaded that we are "post" as in "beyond" rather than "post" as in "recovering from." Shawn grapples with the consequences of global capitalism by presenting violent parables of inequality that make ideology's presence in our lives starkly visible once again.

In Marxian terms, ideology creates false consciousness, blinding us to the relationship between the commodities we purchase on the market and the exploitation of the laborers that produced them. "Ideology" as Althusser elaborates, "has a material existence," a self-reinforcing apparatus comprised of our actions and conventional behaviors.[61] The sudden illness and disaffection of *The Fever*'s speaker can be read as a rupture in the fabric of this apparatus. The unraveling begins when he finds that he can no longer make the gestures of the good bourgeois. For Althusser, ideology does not, as Marx believed, simply cover up "the real." Rather, "[i]deology represents the imaginary relationship of individuals to their real conditions of existence."[62] Following Lacan, Althusser understands our relationship to ideology as always already bounded by language, something we can observe in Shawn's internally riven monologue. The speaker is constituted by his capacity (and incapacity) to explain himself to himself, to his imagined interlocutors, and first his own friends in their apartments in the early 1990s performances, which

---

60 Ibid., 49.
61 Louis Althusser, *Lenin and Philosophy and Other Essays,* trans. Ben Brewster (New York: Monthly Review Press, 2001), 112.
62 Ibid., 109.

Shawn has described as "like a secret meeting of the bourgeois class, in which I would speak frankly about what we were."[63]

A plot can be teased out of *The Fever*, but the play is mainly one long scene of recognition, an unexplained awakening. Marx's *Capital* comes out of nowhere and goes to work not on an intellectual level but as an emetic. Everything is as it was, yet suddenly everything is transfigured. Suddenly, everything is intolerable. There is no event, only knowledge. The postdramatic theatricality of *The Fever*, however, lies in the impossibility of the self coinciding with itself, and the impossibility of the bourgeois self seeing itself, let alone changing itself. Describing the experience of attending a dinner party in a posh quarter of a city much like New York, Shawn's speaker broods over a distinction he would not have been aware of before his awakening. He experiences himself as a person *thinking* about a dinner party, thinking about the complicated feelings he has about the party, about how he likes some of the people, but not others, likes the centerpiece, but not that woman's dress. "But no," he corrects himself, "[n]o. I see it so clearly. I see myself with my little fork — I wasn't a person who was thinking about a party. I was a person who was *at* a party, who sat at the table, drank the wine and ate the fish."[64] The person *thinking* about the party is comprehensible, complicated, sympathetic. The person *at* the party is a George-Grosz caricature of a blasé, cigar-smoking capitalist. The two cannot be reconciled, just as the contradictions of the speaker's life, of all our lives under capitalism cannot be reconciled. The things he loves, the things he lives for, are the same things that make him, him and every member of his class, a murderer and a destroyer of human dignity. There is no reason why he deserves what he has or why the chambermaid deserves her lot, and every day he holds onto what he has, his guilt grows. "Keeping the money is just a choice I'm making, a choice I'm making every day."[65] He could make another choice, the speaker reflects. Why

---

63 Shawn "The Art of Theater No. 17."
64 Shawn, *The Fever*, 6.
65 Ibid., 67.

not give everything away? If people are starving, give them food. Until one is starving oneself, there is no other defensible choice. But the speaker knows he will never make this choice. "The life I live is irredeemably corrupt," he finally concludes, "[i]t has no justification."[66]

If this was Brecht, such recognition would prompt a demand for change, but *The Fever* ends with the newly awakened speaker going back to sleep, choosing private shame over public action. *The Fever* is a peculiar kind of tragedy of waste because the knowledge acquired by the protagonist is wasted, not acted upon. He learns something. He even cares. He is sickened by his knowledge. But Shawn takes a bracingly cynical view of such isolating, unactionable, liberal guilt. There is nothing ennobling about merely feeling bad for the poor or about merely recognizing that the life one lives is irredeemably corrupt. It is only honest, another expression of the privileged, twentieth-century person's narcissistic obsession with self-knowledge. The contained, monologic form of *The Fever* reflects the solipsism of not only a post-ideological but a post-social world. "There is no such thing as society." Without class consciousness, when the collective ceases to exist in the imaginary of the people, collective action becomes impossible, leaving only impotent, misdirected, individual actors presiding over kingdoms of one.

This civic atomization is explored more exhaustively in Shawn's plays featuring multiple characters telling different versions of the same story. *Evening at the Talk House,* Shawn's 2015 play on themes similar to those of *The Fever,* takes place in a post-ideological world that has so thoroughly inoculated itself against conceiving of any alternative to capitalism that it is no longer necessary to keep capitalism's violence entirely hidden from view or fully banned from polite conversation. In the twenty-first century, it is possible for capitalism to go essentially unchallenged, even when fewer and fewer of those who once benefited from the inequalities that capitalism produces are managing to stay on the side of the class divide they feel is their

---

66 Ibid., 64.

birthright, without committing atrocities with their own bare hands. *Talk House* is both a dark fantasia on the emerging gig economy and a referendum on the state of theatrical art, ironically reverting to a more tame, naturalistic dramaturgy even as Shawn is suggesting that as goes the theater, so goes civilization. The demise of this communal art form is imagined as a symptom, or even cause, of a decadent society's descent into barbarism. *Talk House* takes place in the once-tony private club of the play's title, a favorite haunt of theater folk back when that endangered species roamed free. A group of them have reunited to commemorate the ten-year anniversary of a production they worked on together, a highlight in many of their lives. The fortunes of those assembled have risen and fallen unevenly in the ensuing years, but they quickly settle back into familiar habits, trading showbiz snark and memories of the good old days. There is some perfunctory talk about politics, and while certain irregular details, such as the fact that elections are now held every few months though one of the same two candidates always wins, may cause us to prick up our ears, they are not treated as cause for alarm.

Portents of darker developments emerge when the conversation turns to how these erstwhile artists have been scraping together a living now that the theater no longer keeps them in Scotch and hors d'oeuvres. The playwright Robert and leading man Tom have found a measure of success working in television, while the composer Ted and costume designer Annette eventually admit that they have had to take on some freelance work doing "targeting" for the government to supplement their more meager incomes.

"Targeting," Annette insists repeatedly, is "a very simple mechanical process" that happens to involve identifying individuals destined for elimination under the state Program of Murdering.[67] While everyone is aware of the existence of this program, those whose financial circumstances have insulated them from

---

[67] Wallace Shawn, *Evening at the Talk House* (New York: Theatre Communications Group, 2017), 40.

its practical operations are rather shocked to discover that their friends are involved in such things. Annette defends her work and the regular paycheck it guarantees. "I study lists of people and decide who has to be killed," she explains. "Like half the people I know," Ted adds.[68] The murder program might be distasteful, and is for that reason handled secretly, but it is a necessary evil. Annette likens dropping bombs onto people to politely excusing oneself from a meal and "dropping some waste into the toilet."[69] It isn't the done thing to raise such topics in mixed company, but no one denies that they are a part of life.

That this all remains fairly abstract for most people is what makes it possible for the program to exist, but the specter solidifies when formerly beloved actor Dick (played by Shawn in the 2017 US premiere) unexpectedly intrudes on their little party sporting a badly bruised face. He has been beaten by his "friends," a warning issued for expressing unspecified objectionable opinions, and the gossip he has to contribute has to do with mutual acquaintances who have recently dropped dead at dinner, their drinks poisoned by friends in another offshoot of the murder program. Before the *Evening at the Talk House* is out, another life will be claimed in this manner.

How have things reached this point? Where is the resistance? Tom, who hobnobs with the most powerful politicians in the country describes them all as very "nice."[70] The other guests are only concerned with their own comfort and safety. And television ratings. When Jane, a young waitress, shares that she spent time in Nigeria doing some of the murder program's actual murdering, it is remarked that Robert's show isn't at all successful in Nigeria, and the conversation turns to regional tastes in frothy, prime-time offerings. In an introductory soliloquy, Robert admits that he does not really miss the theater, which after all is nothing more than "a small group of humans sitting and star-

---

68 Ibid., 39.
69 Ibid., 37.
70 Ibid., 54.

ing at another small group of humans."[71] This reductive, but not entirely inaccurate, definition sums up much of what is challenging about the theater, what makes it both vital and easily dismissed. It is most often a small-scale operation with a tiny reach compared with film and television. It asks for the sort of sustained and intense attention that makes intimacy possible. It insists on singularity — that of a character trapped in a particular set of circumstances, a director's idiosyncratic way with time and space, or a performer whose heart was pounding a little harder on Friday than on Saturday. It also insists on community, however provisional. We make plays in groups, gather to watch them in groups. Deep knowledge of the other traverses the psychic space between collaborators, and ideally a similar exchange traverses the proscenium. Annette says that she divides her life in two: life before the group's last play together, when her world was shaped by the relationships she cultivated as a theater artist, and life after. Now she sews alone in her apartment doing piecework for wealthy clients. She also does targeting. Society becomes possible when individuals gather together to engage in a wasteful communion. The new scarcity mentality precludes such rites. In *Talk House,* we see social isolation and economic precarity engendering a bourgeoning underclass of contract killers, and we see that the theater will not save us. No, even and especially in the West, the class issue has not actually been successfully resolved.

Elfriede Jelinek, Regietheater, and the Disposable Text

Scholars of postdramatic theater often emphasize the postdramatic's deprivileging of the text, but the Austrian playwright Elfriede Jelinek's plays present the special case of the fully realized, postdramatic text. Jelinek's earliest texts for the theater were scripts, blueprints for productions. They designated characters and dialogue and provided stage directions indicating how speech was intended to drive, conflict with, or otherwise coexist

---

71 Ibid., 10.

with action. In their relatively conventional form, plays such as *Clara S.* (1982), *Illness or Modern Women* (1987), and *Services* (1994) retain readily discernible relationships to narrative causation even though each veers into grotesquerie, with women transforming into vampires in *Illness* and an orgy punched up with bestiality taking over the stage in *Services*. In these texts, though she does not direct her own work, Jelinek took responsibility for the mise-en-scène of her plays. She would establish a passably naturalistic situation and then, over the course of the play, turn it inside-out, rendering latent violence and sexuality manifest. Even in her early plays she always leaves the seams of language showing — characters wear their speech like ill-fitting suits — and this obvious incongruity invites performances that exploit the uneasiness of the speaker's singular physical presence trapped inside a prêt-à-porter vocabulary.

In the German-speaking theater world, however, directors in the *Regietheater* ("director's theater") tradition are the ones who typically take responsibility for ripping plays apart. Jelinek's texts have contributed significantly to tutoring the current generation of major directors in this approach.[72] *Regietheater* is known for aggressive interpretations.[73] Radical cuts, interpolations, transpositions of time and place, and a disregard for the type and number of performers specified by the playwright are all commonplace in the *Regietheater* tradition. This lack of deference to authorial intent and the text itself is distasteful to some, but far from objecting to interventionist approaches to her texts, Jelinek has perhaps uniquely relished tussling with her directors or co-authors. In 1995, the German director Frank Castorf staged a version of *Services* which closed with a staged violation of the body of the author herself — a caricature of Jelinek as a huge, mechanical, sex doll, complete with blinking nipples and genitalia, took the stage and mumbled incomprehensibly

---

72 Gitta Honneger, "Introduction" to Elfriede Jelinek, *Rechnitz and The Merchant's Contracts*, trans. Gitta Honneger (New York: Seagull Books, 2015), 2.
73 Karen Jürs-Munby, "Foreword" to Elfriede Jelinek, *Sports Play*, trans. Penny Black (London: Oberon Books, 2012), 30.

for ten minutes, at once crudely sexualizing Jelinek and making a mockery of the long, digressive, monologic form of her texts. Jelinek approved. Though the choice was offensive, she said, it was absolutely the correct one for the play.

Embracing the fact that, within the *Regietheater* tradition, her texts were bound to be (ab)used as pretexts for the vision of a director, Jelinek began leaving her plays more and more open. Beginning with *Sports Play* in 1998, her prefatory stage directions have been exceedingly minimal and, in tone, ironically resigned to being ignored. "*The author doesn't give many stage directions, she has learned her lesson by now. Do what you like,*" read *Sports Play*'s.[74] In her 2002 "Princess Play," *Jackie,* her initial proposal for a mise-en-scène is followed by the sardonic coda: "But I'm sure you'll think of something completely different."[75] The description of the opening tableau for her 2008 *Rechnitz* concludes more amiably with: "*Of course, it can also be done completely differently, as always with my plays.*"[76] For her 2009 *The Merchant's Contracts* she is particularly blasé: "*The text can start and stop anywhere at random. It doesn't matter how it is staged... whatever...*"[77] Opening stage directions for her 2003 *Bambiland* are comically ornery:

> *I don't know I don't know. Just stick a knit stocking cap on it, the kind with a tassel on top like my dad used to wear with his old overalls while building our little single-family home. Never seen anything uglier than that. I don't know what kind of crime you'd have to commit or sentence you'd have to get to get stuck wearing something that ugly on your head. Cut off a knit stocking, tie it off at the top to form a sort of pom-pom, and stick it on your head. That's that.*[78]

---

74 Jelinek, *Sports Play,* 39.
75 Elfriede Jelinek, *Princess Plays: Jackie, Theater* 36, no. 2 (2006): 53.
76 Jelinek, *Rechnitz and The Merchant's Contracts,* 64.
77 Ibid., 176.
78 Elfriede Jelinek, *Bambiland, Theater* 39, no. 3 (2009): 111.

She sounds as though she has just been asked for guidance by an incompetent costume designer who has been pestering her for hints all morning. The answer she gives is characteristically confounding. Willfully obscure, saying too little of what is necessary to efficiently convey meaning and too much of what seems extraneous, opaque, inappropriately autobiographical, and glib. "Like my dad used to wear" does not provide the director or reader with an objective description or image of any kind. It is a hopelessly personal association. The author's affect overwhelms her content. Communication is subordinated to attitude.

In each of these cases, Jelinek is at once provoking directors, confronting them with a challenge, and surrendering to their authority. She provokes by writing texts that are often literally unstageable as written. Too long, too formless, and too impenetrable, her texts for the theater have been called "language planes" (*Textflächen*). "Since the drama in her texts does not unfold in the action," her frequent translator Gitta Honegger writes, "but is buried in the language itself — quotes from literary and philosophical canons, from historical sources, popular culture, political speak, and the Web — it is up to the directors of Jelinek's plays to cull the narrative they will stage from the 150-odd pages of texts."[79] This type of challenge also presents enormous opportunities; a director has a great deal of leeway when it comes to determining what in the text they would like to emphasize or deemphasize, criticize, mock, ignore, or cut (indeed, in most cases, they must cut simply to wrestle a piece down to a manageable scale. Einer Schleef's landmark 1998 production of *Sports Play* included 142 performers and lasted seven hours, an undertaking that very few theaters would have the resources to support. Regarding the necessity of imposing cuts on a Jelinek play, the director Nicholas Stemann once said that "[y]ou don't cut it with a pencil as with other theatre texts where you may draw some lines. No, with Jelinek's texts you have to cut with a machete [*einer Schleef*]!"[80] While the notion of the "open"

---

79 Honegger, "Introduction," 2.
80 Quoted in Jürs-Munby, "Foreword," 33.

or porous text for the stage has become more and more ubiquitous and accepted, especially in the German-speaking area, Jelinek goes even further in her willingness to allow her texts to be treated as assemblages of waste, where nothing is deemed essential, no constituent part of a text deemed more important than any other. Chop them up and cast aside hours' worth of material and so long as the texture of her texts remains, they still accomplish the work of imaginative resistance that they were designed to do, offering themselves up as metaphors for the very culture of overconsumption and disposability in which they were produced.

The Merchant's Contracts: Shoveling Shit

Where Shawn's vision of late capitalism is one of violence perpetuated by depression, Jelinek's is one of violence perpetuated by desire. In her "Comedy of Economics," *The Merchant's Contracts,* Jelinek takes on modern finance capitalism, where capital's movements need not be tethered to anything so twentieth-century mundane as the production of goods. Capital can now exist in a state of near-total abstraction aided by, as Fredric Jameson points out, "the intensification of communications technology to the point at which capital transfers today abolish space and time, virtually instantaneously effectuated across national spaces."[81] *Contracts* was written in response to an Austrian scandal. The unscrupulous investment practices of two trusted Austrian financial institutions led to many small investors losing their life savings. The script was completed just a few weeks before Lehman Brothers in the US filed for bankruptcy in 2008, setting off the global financial crisis and instantly enhancing the resonance of Jelinek's text. "In the age of global economy," as Honegger puts it, "Jelinek turned the merchant of Vienna into a universal comedy of errors."[82]

---

81 Fredric Jameson, "Culture and Finance Capital," *Critical Inquiry* 24, no. 1 (1997): 252.
82 Honegger, "Introduction," 20.

Necessity seemed to demand leaving *Contracts* more open than any Jelinek text to date, given the events rapidly unfolding in the financial sector and around the world. Director Nicholas Stemann developed an open-ended dramaturgy that allowed for the interweaving of up-to-the minute topical material so that the production could keep up with cascading current events. In the main section of the text, which Jelinek titles "The Real Thing," money and those who possess the mystical power to make more of it, to make something from nothing, are repeatedly referred to as "doing God's work." For the 2009 premiere in Cologne, Jelinek wrote an epilogue taking into account the Lehman Brothers debacle in which she portrays speculative capitalism run amok, "Capitalism as Dionysus."[83] This is a different kind of god, a god of excess, a god who gives his blessing to those who risk much and lose control. "Capitalism is the only power we must acknowledge," the bacchants/investors intone, "[w]e don't exist without it. How else should we distinguish ourselves from the other? How else to use ourselves as weapons? Wouldn't that mean even more violence? That without capitalism we would not be?"[84] He moves in mysterious ways.

In subsequent productions of *Contracts,* different cuts, additions, and rearrangements continued to be made as the effects of the churning economic catastrophe continued to ripple out. Though the uncut text clocked in at over five hours, Stemann decided to make only minimal cuts. Given the staggering volume of text and the incessant revisions, actors performed with scripts in hand and Stemann himself directing traffic onstage. Sections of text were delivered at a frenetic, sometimes incomprehensible pace, sometimes overlapping, and in a variety of conflicting styles. "If it is impossible to grasp the entire text this way," Honegger writes, "its frantic performance reflects the degree society is able (or unable) to absorb the onslaught of stock market lingo (an unintelligible language for most)."[85]

---

83 Jelinek, *Rechnitz and The Merchant's Contracts,* 285.
84 Ibid.
85 Honegger, "Introduction," 29.

It was to be assumed that much of the language would remain inaccessible to audiences, that it would be thrown away, wasted from a syntactical point of view, from the standpoint of efficient communication. As Honegger rightly points out, the highly specialized jargon of the financial industry is impenetrable to most. The financial services sector depends on this jargon alienating laymen, making them feel intimidated enough to turn their portfolio over to a wealth manager or their taxes over to an accountant. Intimidating inscrutability is good for business — without it, few would be willing to pay a fee to someone who knows how to navigate the thicket and promises to score their client a good deal. The *Textflächen* of finance contribute to enormous discrepancies between top insiders and those whose money they play with. The voices in *Contracts* rise and fall between the small investors for whom a nest egg meant a livelihood, a home, retirement and the speculators for whom the small investors are just another abstraction, like money. People don't work. Money works. You are only as valuable as the capital you are willing to part with, so that your money can work for other people.

One of the local scandals that inspired *Contracts* concerned the beleaguered Bank for Labor and Business, which belonged to the Austrian Labor Union but was purchased by an American company, Cerberus Capital Management, after coming close to collapse. This gave Jelinek a useful associative starting point. In Greek mythology, Cerberus is the three-headed hound that guards the gates of the underworld for his master, Hades. Capturing Cerberus was the last of the twelve labors of Hercules, which he was pressed to perform in order to atone for murdering his wife and children in a fit of madness. The financial crisis produced an Austrian echo of this fabled horror as well, and Jelinek duly appropriated it. In 2008 a Viennese public relations manager who had lost all his family's money in toxic stocks purchased an axe. He killed his wife and seven-year-old daughter, then drove to a neighboring town, killed his parents, then drove to another town and killed his father-in-law. He planned to kill himself but lost his nerve after realizing that it took at least thirteen blows of the axe for each of his victims to expire.[86]

But Jelinek does not organize the text around the capture of Cerberus or around the little guy who has been duped by the powerful exacting his revenge against all odds. Jelinek focuses on the fifth labor, when Hercules was sent to King Augeas, owner of more cattle than anyone in Greece, and told that he had to clean the king's stables in a single day. Hercules told the king that he would perform this amazing feat if Augeas would give him one tenth of his precious cattle. Certain that what Hercules had proposed couldn't be done, King Augeas agreed. Hercules tore great openings in opposite walls of the stables, dug wide trenches to two nearby rivers, redirecting them so that they flowed through the stables, flushing out all the animal waste. Though he had succeeded, cleaning the Augean stables was deemed not to "count," because Hercules had accepted payment for his labor.

In *Contracts,* the shit is debt, the buying and selling and leveraging of which has come to undergird much of modern finance. For a performance in 2010, Jelinek wrote another epilogue titled "You Bet! (A Sequel)" in a which a figure designated as "I or Another Animal" celebrates: "Isn't that dandy, something is coming from nothing […]. The shit's coming too, there it is, it always comes."[87] While the financiers are moving vast amounts of imaginary money around at dizzying speeds, the subprime mortgage crisis hits, and real people who bet on their real homes find that everything they thought they had is worthless. "[T]hat's only human that debts turn into shit, that everything turns into shit, that most of all money turns into shit, that money already IS shit before it's even there, but it's never there when it's needed."[88]

---

86 "Lebenslange Haft für fünffachen Axtmörder" ["Life Sentence for Five-Time Ax Murderer"], *Spiegel Online,* November 7, 2008, https://www.spiegel.de/panorama/justiz/wien-lebenslange-haft-fuer-fuenffachen-axtmoerder-a-589185.html.
87 Jelinek, *Rechnitz and The Merchant's Contracts,* 322.
88 Ibid.

In *Contracts* the shit keeps piling up, debt that suddenly no one can profit from, but in a further, grotesque twist, Jelinek has the sewer system that is the Augean stables that is the global debt market mortgaged, itself held hostage now that even the callous creditors have seen their money disappear. Finally, no one gets bailed out. There is not enough liquidity, only constipation:

> Okay, it would have to pay, if the owner of the shit processing plant would have to pay, but he doesn't have to either, he has to take a shit, but he doesn't have to pay. We all have to shit, but no one wants to pay for it and no one has to, if he's already taken his shit and making a shitload, he doesn't have to take any more shit, he won't poop or pay, it's been paid for, it paid for itself, and now no one will pay.[89]

Jelinek's comedy of economics has antecedents in the simpler, more straightforwardly scatological fare that dominated the Parisian boulevards when mercantilism still represented a relatively new world order. A short 1756 farce by Thomas-Simon Gueullette titled "The Shit Merchant" shows a Harlequin figure tricking the naïf Gilles into believing that he can make a killing selling his own excrement. Desperate for cash, Gilles makes a spectacle of himself touting this allegedly hot commodity around the fairground, crying, "[w]ho wants my shit? Money for my shit! It's fresh."[90] Gilles is a figure of ridicule, but he is also tragic, in Artaud's sense, reduced to the most basic and base of human functions. "There where it smells of shit," Artaud writes, "it smells of being."[91] Must eat to shit. Must shit to eat. Capitalism, however complex, reveals itself in Gueullete's burlesque to be modeled on this very cycle of abjection and incorporation.

---

89 Ibid., 304.
90 Thomas-Simon Gueullette, "Le Marchand du Merde," in *Théatre des boulevards, ou Recueil de parades,* ed. A. Mahon (Paris: De l'imprimerie de Gilles Langlois, 1756), 255. Translation mine.
91 Antonin Artaud, *Antonin Artaud: Selected Writings,* ed. Susan Sontag (Los Angeles: University of California Press, 1988), 559.

In Jelinek's play, "streams of capital and shit" are said to flow together indistinguishably. Few can separate them. Most drink from the wrong source and get poisoned.

Only an elite, priestly caste can decipher the signs of collapse or revival; they are said to be able to read the language of God. In *Contracts* a number of Angels answer the lamentations of a chorus of small investors. The Angel of Justice begins to sermonize: "[l]abor is the source of all wealth and all culture," she says, "and since profitable labor is only possible in society and through society, the yield of labor belongs wholly, with equal rights for all, to all members of society."[92] But she loses faith in her message half way through her speech: "None of this is true, not true, any of it, none of it true [...]?"[93] Since "wealth" has become an unrecognizable category, some fluctuating combination of toxic debt and abstract credit, "growth" comes to replace the old markers of stability and prosperity. More angels intercede to palliate the Angel of Justice's socialist logic with a ringing, triumphalist battle hymn of neoliberalism:

> Those are the essences, those are the essentials of a truly free country, all our freedoms depend upon this freedom. We want a totally free economy, not only because it guarantees freedoms, but because it is the best way to create wealth and prosperity for the entire country, for Europe, for the country which has our name and is us! Wealth is the single resource for our growth, no, for your growth, no, for everyone's growth, for wealth in itself is thriving, but only when it grows, when it increases, when it grows, right, no? Right![94]

While this seraphic choir sings of eternal glory, its appearance, as in the Book of Revelation, is a harbinger of the apocalypse. The growth they praise is death.

---

92 Ibid., 243.
93 Ibid.
94 Ibid., 262.

2

War: Abjection and Oblivion

Georges Bataille interprets the first artistic gesture as an apology for human existence. Much of human endeavor can be understood as an extension of that impulse. Through successive ages of imperialism, it has appeared as though Western man's greatest ambition was dominion over all things, but our present model of suicide capitalism suggests that the goal of ever-accelerating growth has always been to spend ourselves as quickly as possible, to destroy ourselves and cease to be.

Before Freud accepted the death drive, he saw most self-generated impediments to human pleasure-seeking as perversions. These developmental detours yielded types of pleasure that existed outside normative or efficient economies of pleasure production. Freud believed that childhood anal eroticism, a fixation on the giving or withholding of one's waste products, could help explain the formation of neurotic adult personality characteristics. During the anal stage of psychosexual development, a child prone to erotic stimulation of the anal zone may display a tendency to obstinately hold back his waste, sometimes waiting to empty his bowels until doing so will cause maximum inconvenience for his caretaker. In this early phase of life, this exercise of control is one of the few available to the child. In exerting control over his physiological functions, the child rehearses the control he will later seek to exercise over other areas of his life.

"The contents of the bowels," Freud says, are "treated as part of the infant's own body and represent his first 'gift:' by producing them he can express his active compliance with his environment and, by withholding them, his disobedience."[1] The child uses the (mis)management of his waste products as an instrument of perverse control, but also identifies himself with those very waste products. His waste represents his first opportunity to exercise his will, to assert himself as *homo faber*. It is his first experience of power, both as an autonomous agent with the ability to refuse and as a creator of a thing of value, albeit of dubious value — Freud points out that gold, or mammon, has since archaic times appeared as allied with, or as a stand-in for, the feces of the devil. Freud also speculates that it may be "the contrast between the most precious substance known to men and the most worthless, which they reject as waste matter ('refuse'),[that] has led to [the] identification of gold with faeces."[2] According to Freud, anality comes to shape the adult personality in an unhealthy way when the child emerges from his negotiation with the conflicts presented during the toilet-training phase with either anal-retentive or anal-expulsive tendencies, either too parsimonious or overly unregulated in his behavior. It is the conflict itself, however, that is formative — man comes to esteem himself first through denial and abasement, through a confrontation with himself as a creator of that which is vile.

Julia Kristeva reads this primal gift-giving as the archetypical site of abjection, the process of constructing identity via the casting-off of that which is considered so repugnant or intolerable that its proximity infringes on the subject's sense of self, threatening dissolution and incoherence. "What is abject," she writes, "is not my correlative, which, providing me with someone or something else as support, would allow me to be more or less detached and autonomous. The abject has only one qual-

---

1   Sigmund Freud, *Three Essays on the Theory of Sexuality*, ed. and trans. James Strachey (New York: Basic Books, 1962), 52.
2   Sigmund Freud, "Character and Anal Eroticism," in *The Freud Reader*, ed. Peter Gay, trans. James Strachey (New York: Norton & Co., 1989), 297.

ity of the object — that of being opposed to *I*."[3] Abjection plays a critical role in ego-formation on both the individual and the cultural levels. We abject various racial, religious, and sexual others to shore up the integrity of the unmarked *I*. Those construed as waste products are not discarded, but rather must remain present in the imaginary as crucial to personal or cultural integrity. This integrity is contingent on boundaries, division, retention, and control — anal-retentive personality characteristics that stand in sharp contrast to the primal yearning Bataille sees in the artifacts of prehistoric man, who experienced the individuation of his species with shame. Early man's emerging distance from the animal world, the barrier sealing him off from nature, gave him pain, not comfort. Though we may have forgotten the origin of that pain, Bataille would argue, one has only to behold the orgy of self-destruction we have made of the modern world to see that everything in the human still aches to return to insentience. "Today's man suspects the inanity of the edifice he has founded, he knows that he knows nothing," Bataille writes, "and, as his ancestors concealed their features with animal masks, he summons the night of truth wherein the world that has ordained his pretension will cease being *clear* and *distinct*."[4] The "night of truth" is war; if barriers must exist, man will annihilate them through violence.

Heiner Müller, Hapless Angel

In a famous passage from his "Theses on the Philosophy of History," Walter Benjamin describes the Klee painting *Angelus Novus*, which

> shows an angel looking as though he is about to move away from something he is fixedly contemplating. His eyes are

---

[3] Julia Kristeva, *Powers of Horror: An Essay on Abjection,* trans. Leon S. Roudiez (New York: Columbia University Press, 1982), 1.

[4] Georges Bataille, *The Cradle of Humanity: Prehistoric Art and Culture,* trans. Stuart Kendall (New York: Zone Books, 2005), 80.

> staring, his mouth is open, his wings are spread. This is how one pictures the angel of history. His face is turned toward the past. Where we perceive a chain of events, he sees one single catastrophe which keeps piling wreckage upon wreckage and hurls it in front of his feet. The angel would like to stay, awaken the dead, and make whole what has been smashed. But a storm is blowing from Paradise; it has got caught in his wings with such violence that the angel can no longer close them. This storm irresistibly propels him into the future to which his back is turned, while the pile of debris before him grows skyward. This storm is what we call progress.[5]

A progressive theory of history holds that human history is marching inexorably towards the good, toward liberty and justice for all. Fukuyama's theory of history is in this sense progressive. Benjamin wonders whether the costs of so-called progress are really worth the benefits. In Benjamin's bleak vision, the call of progress tears us away from the work of healing, reintegration, of making "whole what has been smashed." The angel wants to repair the disastrous errors of the past, but the storm of progress bears him backward into the future to witness new disasters piling onto the old. The heap of debris grows much faster than anyone could possibly sift through it to bring out the bodies, but even if that were not the case only an angel could be expected to awaken the dead, the waste of history.

Heir to Brecht's legacy, the East German playwright and director Heiner Müller did not share his artistic progenitor's faith in revolutionary progress. His vision of history owed more to Benjamin. In a 1958 piece of text called "The Hapless Angel," Müller revisits Benjamin's Angel of History:

> Behind him the past washes ashore, piles debris on his wings and shoulders, with the noise of buried drums, while before him the future dams up, impresses itself down on

---

5 Walter Benjamin, *Illuminations: Essays and Reflections,* trans. Harry Zorn, ed. Hannah Arendt (New York: Schocken Books, 1969), 257–58.

his eyes, bursts his eyeballs like a star, twists his words into a sounding muzzle, chokes him with its breath. For a time one can still see the beating of his wings, hear into the roar the landslide coming down before above behind him, louder the more furious his futile movement, sporadic as it languishes. Then the moment closes down over him: standing, buried by debris quickly, the hapless angel comes to rest, waiting for history in the petrification of flight glance breath. Until the renewed roar of mighty beating wings propagates itself in undulations through the stone and announces his flight.[6]

In Müller's version, the angel is not merely forced to *behold* the ugly spectacle of the wrecked past's waste piling up in the name of progress; he is being buried alive by it. What is more, the angel is being pulverized from both sides. Not only the past, but the future, oppresses him. Brecht adopted the writings of Marx and Lenin as gospel; he believed that the coming global socialist utopia would deliver all of suffering humanity to salvation. Müller's faith in alternatives to capitalism was undermined by the gap between the utopian ambitions of communist movements and the gruesome reality of what the Soviet experiment produced. For the Hapless Angel, the way forward is dammed, the future as irredeemably damned as the past. Benjamin's Angel experienced progress as a storm; he does not know or dream of where he is being borne. He is powerless, but at least he is spared the torture of imagination. In contrast, Müller's Angel's eyes explode as expectations, aspirations, unrealized plans accumulate. Blind and immobilized, the angel, like progress, is gridlocked. His wings flap uselessly.

After the fall of the Berlin Wall, Müller returned to the image once again with a short poem he titled "Hapless Angel 2." Here, the Angel is unmoored, unknown, and unknowable:

---

6 Heiner Müller, "Hapless Angel," cited in Helen Fehervary, "Enlightenment or Entanglement: History and Aesthetics in Bertolt Brecht and Heiner Müller," *New German Critique* 8 (1976): 93.

> Between city and city
> After the wall the abyss
> Wind at the shoulders the alien
> Hand at the lonely flesh
> The angel I still hear him
> Yet he has no face anymore but
> Yours that I don't know[7]

The Angel, like the speaker of the poem, suffers from rootlessness, isolation, and lack of either identity or direction. Long skeptical about revolutions and critical of revolutionaries, Müller recognizes that without a cause projecting him into a future, the angel is lost.

Revolution as Theater/Theater as Revolution

Modern tragedy, Raymond Williams posits, is grounded in the awareness of the need for continuous revolution. To be modern is to be in the midst of constant flux, a permanent state of shattering and rebuilding. To see this state as tragic is to take into account the violence and destruction, the inevitable waste that revolution entails. In the *post*modern era, we are afflicted with what Kristeva calls "postmodern forgetting." Facing a crisis of subjectivity and a crisis of knowledge, we struggle to maintain an unequivocal link to our cultural stories, to the truth of past atrocities. We buckle under the unbearable lightness of ahistoricity. Nietzsche tells us that

> in the smallest and greatest happiness there is always one thing that makes it happiness: the power of forgetting, or, in more learned phrase, the capacity of feeling "unhistorically" throughout its duration. One who cannot leave himself behind on the threshold of the moment and forget the past, who cannot stand on a single point, like a goddess of victory, without fear or giddiness, will never know what happiness is;

7 Ibid., 57.

and, worse still, will never do anything to make others happy.[8]

But the practice of "active forgetting," advocated by Nietzsche, can be either the instrument or the downfall of those engaged in the modern project of revolution. "Revolution" can mean an insurrection, but the word can also be used, as Kristeva uses it, to refer to a *turn,* an instance of revolving completed by a *re*turn to one's original position.

When questioned on the subject, Müller was known to scoff, "[r]evolution? After the next ice age." Müller based several of his own most nihilistic plays on Brecht's optimistic, utilitarian *Lehrstücke* plays. Variously translated as "teaching plays," "learning plays," or "didactic plays," the *Lehrstücke* were intended to be performed only by and for groups of workers engaged in the process of educating themselves. They were to be tools for cultivating revolutionary consciousness, not aesthetic objects to be passively consumed. As Andrzej Wirth and Marta Ulvaeus describe it, in the *Lehrstücke* project, "two utopian concepts meet: the theater as metatheater, and society as changeable. [...] [T]heater should function without an audience, society without classes."[9] No longer would the proscenium divide those who produced from those who consumed, perniciously duplicating the oppressive social dynamics of the world outside the theater. The *Lehrstücke* erase the divide between producers and consumers. The worker/performers own the means of production and labor for their own benefit, no one else's. The plots of the plays pose intellectual and moral dilemmas analogous to those workers might be expected to confront on the road to revolution. They conclude with a resolution intended to be instructive, an outcome to be emulated. The *Lehrstücke* are plays that are ex-

8 Friedrich Nietzsche, *On the Use and Abuse of History for Life,* trans. Adrian Collins (New York: Cosimo, 2005), 6.
9 Ardrzej Wirth and Marta Ulvaeus, "The Lehrstück as Performance," TDR: *The Drama Review* 43, no. 4 (1999): 113.

pected to perform a function, rather than merely be performed. Theirs is a functionalist dramaturgy.

In Brecht's *The Measures Taken*, for example, four communist agitators return from China and relate to their central committee in Moscow the sacrifice they found it necessary to make in order to complete their mission successfully. The action of the play is related, not enacted. In China their young fifth comrade, so distressed by the injustice he witnessed, was moved to shortsighted, indiscreet acts of compassion that threatened to jeopardize their contingent's larger goals. Ultimately, with his assent, the agitators decide to protect their cause by shooting the young comrade and disposing of his body in a lime pit. The central committee commends them for having done the right thing under the circumstances.

Müller responded to *The Measures Taken* in 1970 with *Mauser*, a relentlessly bleak, cyclical variation on Brecht's themes. Barred from being either performed or published in the German Democratic Republic (GDR), *Mauser* also focuses on the problem of the loyal revolutionary who goes rogue. Loyalty is not an all-or-nothing proposition; in Brecht's play, the young comrade believes so deeply in his party's cause that he cannot delay the instant gratification he experiences helping the downtrodden for the sake of later, larger victories for the oppressed. In Müller's version, a revolutionary charged with killing enemies of the revolution becomes so zealous in discharging his duties that the violence spins out of control. He begins killing for the pure love of killing and must finally agree to be killed himself for the sake of the revolution. Like *The Measures Taken*, *Mauser* is designed to be performed without an inactive audience. It is a play for doing, not for seeing. In a note appended to the published text, Müller explains that *Mauser*

> is not a play for the repertoire; [...] Performance for an audience is possible if the audience is invited to control the performance by its text, and the text by its performance, through reading the Chorus part, or the part of the First Player (A), or if the Chorus part is read by one group of spectators and the

part of the First Player by another group of spectators — the text not read by each group should be blotted out in the script — or through other devices; and if the audience's reaction can be controlled through the non-synchronism of text and performance, the nonidentity of speaker and performer. The proposed distribution of the text is variable, the mode and degree of variants a political choice that has to be made in each individual case.[10]

The first part of this instruction is straightforward enough. Müller more or less explains the way a *Lehrstück* works. The piece is not to be performed for a traditional, passive, segregated audience. The second part is more ambiguous, the notion of the audience's reaction being "controlled" feels vaguely sinister and decidedly un-Brechtian. Brecht used "the non-synchronism of text and performance" to cultivate the estranging *Verfremdungseffekt*, but Müller's work is addressed to a pre-alienated audience. He does not seek to use his "teaching plays" to teach through appeals to reason. Instead, he carries the dialectical process to the point of absurdity and collapse. *Mauser* is a crushingly elliptical text. Though Müller leaves it to the performer/spectators to cast themselves in various roles, we always come back to the play's refrain: "DEATH TO THE ENEMIES OF THE REVOLUTION." The play is a machine, grinding into gruel its initially distinct speakers. Speeches are assigned to the following entities:

– Chorus
– A
– A(Chorus)
– B
– Chorus(The Performers of Three Farmers)
– Chorus(A)

---

10 Heiner Müller, *Mauser*, in *A Heiner Müller Reader: Plays, Poetry, Prose*, ed. and trans. Carl Weber (Baltimore: Johns Hopkins University Press, 2001), 106.

The casting choices may initially seem meaningful, with guilt being apportioned unequally among the speakers, some bearing more responsibility than others, some representing the pragmatic perspective and others held up as exemplars of a fallacy. The play begins as a fairly lucid dialogue between the Chorus and A, the revolutionary, being indicted for his misconduct:

> A: I have done my work.
> CHORUS: Do your last one.
> A: I have killed for the Revolution.
> CHORUS: Die for her.
> A: I have committed a mistake.
> CHORUS: You are the mistake.
> A: I am a human being.
> CHORUS: What is that.[11]

By the time we receive an answer to this question, it is considerably less clear who is on whose side, who is speaking on whose behalf, who is indicting whom, on what grounds and to what purpose. According to the text, the chorus volunteers the delayed response itself. "A man," the chorus says, "is something you shoot into / Until Man will rise from the ruins of man."[12] The individual must be destroyed so that the collective might thrive. The real must be annihilated so that the ideal might arise. Violent as the imagery is, this poetic assessment sounds like the sort of slogan that could conceivably be endorsed by sane people in desperate times who take seriously their dreams for a better tomorrow. But Müller puts into the mouths of each of his designated speakers a related refrain that topples the Tatlinesque tower of progressive pipe dreams into the blood-soaked soil: "[k]nowing, even the grass / We must tear up so it will stay green."[13] This, of course, is madness.

---

11 Müller, *Mauser*, 95.
12 Ibid., 103.
13 Ibid., 95.

The American sculptor Justin Matherly adopts this line as the title for one of a series of his pieces fashioned from concrete and ambulatory equipment. This particular sculpture consists of a vaguely humanoid mass of concrete perched precariously on a pair of hospital-style walkers. The patient is not intact — only a pair of hollowed-out stumps of thighs attached to a scarred, bulging torso remain. Already denuded of its organicity by the material (concrete being, eloquently, a kind of man-made stone), what remains of this "body" has been fused to what appear to be woefully inadequate mechanical substitutes for that which has been lost. The form of the sculpture is based on the Belvedere Torso, the famous fragment of ancient Greek sculpture that profoundly influenced Michelangelo and other Renaissance artists when it was brought to the Vatican in 1523. What Michelangelo so admired about that piece was the sense of tension and internal struggle it captured. During the Renaissance, humanism flourished as Europe emerged from the Dark Ages and rediscovered the art and writings of classical antiquity. As interest in the general value and goodness of the human gradually overtook the narrow religious focus of medieval scholasticism, man was "reborn" as the center of the known universe. The Enlightenment idea that through the application of their powers of reason men were destined to become the "masters and possessors of nature" followed.[14] Under the stewardship of mankind in its rush to realize this goal, what we call nature has not fared well. This is despite the fact that, as posthumanist thinkers have shown, human beings are not in any meaningful way separate from nature, a category of our own invention, nor have we managed to escape the deleterious effects of our attempts to exert dominance over it. Matherly's useless mass of wrecked flesh reflects on the foundering of the Cartesian proposition, the breakdown of the anthropocentric worldview.

Like the play from which it is transposed, Matherly's sculpture is a queasy-making admission that humankind has lost

---

14 René Descartes, *Discourse on Method and Meditations* (New York: The Liberal Arts Press), 45.

control. The rampaging revolutionary "A" in *Mauser* loses it by hubristically assuming too much control. "DEATH TO THE ENEMIES OF THE REVOLUTION" becomes a suicide slogan when the speakers start to become confused and conflated—A(Chorus) and Chorus(A)?—and it becomes clear that there are ultimately *only* enemies of the revolution. Loyalty expires. Killing becomes "a science," "work like any other work," and "daily bread."[15] Jonathan Kalb observes that in this post-Stalinist nightmare, the factory, that once-glorified symbol of the revolutionary Soviet state, becomes a slaughterhouse. "Here the vision is of production and death, production *of* death."[16] The revolution tears up grass and grinds up bodies, laying waste to man and insensate matter alike. Even more so than *Mother Courage, Mauser* can be described as an allegory of pure waste. No new Man grows out of the ruined bodies of men, no new city on a hill out of the ruins of the old, no hope out of despair. Revolution as a turn or return is a zero-sum game, but no one profits in *Mauser*. Not even a little cache of blood money remains to be divided among the victors. It is impossible even to tell who the victors are or if, indeed, there are any.

Bonnie Marranca calls Müller's *Lehrstücke* "unlearning plays."[17] Revisiting his source material again and again, cannibalizing Brecht's texts and his own in as many ways as he knows how, Müller gives the impression that, like Beckett, he cannot rest until he has devoured language with language. Where Beckett courts silence, Müller is after a total denaturing of language. Both orbit aporias, but where for Beckett memory is, like speech, emptied out, Müller's utterances are shards of literary allusions, ideological statements, and images of violence, dereliction, and disgust breaking off and tumbling down from the slag heap of German history. Heidi Schlipphacke asserts that, *pace* Kristeva, Germany and Austria suffer from "precisely a lack

---

15 Müller, *Mauser,* 98, 96, 100.
16 Jonathan Kalb, *The Theater of Heiner Müller* (New York: Limelight Editions, 2001), 53.
17 Bonnie Marranca, *Ecologies of Theater* (Baltimore: The Johns Hopkins University Press, 1996), 71.

of 'forgetting.'"[18] In these countries where the historical break of the Holocaust occurred, marking their regression to premodernity, national identity remains onerously intact as compared with the rest of globalizing, postmodern Europe. In Germany and Austria there is too much history, too much memory, too much of the "I" and its painful associations. Müller plays the role of a sadistic psychoanalyst who puts his traumatized patient on the couch, dragging them through the hell of recollection and ripping them apart without having any intention of putting them back together again. Even Freud cautioned against fullblown, psychotic individuals submitting to analysis — the process of self-excavation is difficult and painful, and patients have a tendency to get worse before they get better. Sifting through the detritus of Germany's collective unconscious, Müller never arrives at a moment when the possibility of recovered integrity seems within reach for his analysand. Instead, his plays frequently "give up" on themselves, pivoting to an imagined other for salvation.

In Müller's *The Task,* this "other" is, broadly construed, what used to be called the Third World. Written nine years after *Mauser, The Task* is another version of *The Measures Taken,* but its agitators are beset not by an excess of zeal, but by a sense of exhaustion, redundancy, and nullification. Three emissaries from the French National Convention — Galloudec, Sasportas, and Debuisson — are sent to colonial Jamaica to incite a slave rebellion against the British just as the coup of 18 Brumaire is taking place at home. With Napoleon ascending to power, effectively ending the French Revolution, the mission drifts. "The revolution has no home anymore," Debuisson says, "what we believed to be the dawn of freedom was maybe only the mask of a new, even more hideous slavery."[19] But on the precipice of this aporia, the uncountenanceable thought that the struggle

18 Heidi M. Schlipphacke, *Nostalgia after Nazism: History, Home, and Affect in German and Austrian Literature and Film* (Lewisburg: Bucknell University Press, 2010), 75.
19 Heiner Müller, *Hamletmachine and Other Texts for the Stage,* ed. and trans. Carl Weber (New York: PAJ, 1984), 98.

might have been in vain, Debuisson attempts to re-center the revolution by designating for it a new homeland. He dreams of walking through a run-down, minority neighborhood in New York and seeing omens of the next iteration of the struggle rise up like hallucinations on the city sidewalk. A golden serpent represents Asia. A radiant blue serpent represents Africa. These will be the next frontiers of the revolution. Debuisson has had enough of seeing his loves Liberty, Equality, and Fraternity whored out, dragged through "all the sewers of this world, [...] all the brothels."[20] Pure revolutionary ideals have been used to justify all manner of atrocities. Equality has been embraced by every repressive regime. Fraternity has been exploited by murderers everywhere. Every dictator has put his lips to Liberty's breast. "For a thousand years our three loves have been laughed at," Debuisson laments, "now I want to sit where they laugh, free to do anything that's to my taste, equal to myself, my own, and no one else's brother."[21]

Dead ends and disillusionment culminate in scornful abdication and satanic laughter. As Baudelaire put it, laughter is "born of Man's conception of his own superiority. Since it is essentially human, it is also essentially contradictory, that is to say it is at once the sign of infinite grandeur and of infinite wretchedness."[22] For Baudelaire, laughter as an expression of superiority to nature is the pride that goeth before destruction, as the haughty spirit before a fall. There will ultimately be no safe outside space set aside for retired insurrectionists to remain aloof, to laugh from a distance as the colonized world convulses. Though the speakers in *The Mission* maintain somewhat more characterological continuity than those in *Mauser* they are still the mouthpieces of a dizzying range of contradictions. Debuisson is blasé, even cruel one moment, laughing satanically at the dirty, brown people scrambling up behind the Europeans to set

20 Ibid., 99.
21 Ibid.
22 Charles Baudelaire, *The Essence of Laughter and Other Essays, Journals, and Letters,* ed. Peter Quennell (New York: Meridian Books, 1956), 117.

Revolution 3.0 in motion, then he is confiding tremblingly to his comrades that he is "afraid […] of the beauty of the world. I know very well," he says, "it is the mask of treason. […] I am afraid […] of the shame to be happy in this world."[23] The impulsive, unruly compassion of Brecht's young comrade has aged, grown into jaundiced, unactionable shame. Happiness is betrayal for Debuisson because it perverts time and space. It is the point at which myth becomes history. Embodied man is only hopeful because he is always forgetting, in Nietzsche's sense, always in the present tense. Müller ends the play with Debuisson retreating into the temporary eternity and the finite infinity of a lover's embrace. Like Liberty, Equality, and Fraternity, Betrayal is a woman. Debuisson covers his ears and succumbs to the embrace of betrayal, who throws herself on him "like a heaven, the bliss of the labia at dawn."[24]

Woman is the horizon, the vanishing point. "In Müller's work," Bonnie Marranca observes, "Woman is spirit, nature, womb, Plato's cave, the black hole in space, a prison, a snakepit, a one-way street. She is also the landscape of utopia, his grand theme."[25] By making Woman into everything, he reduces her to nothing. Conjured as a dream or a nightmare, the reality of whatever she might be will always seem crude, mean, offensive. In Müller's work, "Woman, like nature," Marranca argues, "is made to embody the ideology of the eternal feminine, passive, fated. But nature is not a still life, nor is the earth a receptacle."[26] When Woman finally speaks, in defiance of this enforced symbolic passivity, she must cut through centuries of images that have been projected onto her by men.

---

23 Müller, *Hamletmachine*, 100.
24 Ibid., 101.
25 Marranca, *Ecologies of Theater*, 77.
26 Ibid.

Elfriede Jelinek: Trümmerfrau of Language

Elfriede Jelinek suffers from acute anxiety and seldom leaves her home near the edge of the Vienna Woods. When she won the Nobel Prize for Literature in 2004, she did not attend the ceremony, citing agoraphobia, instead delivering her address via a tape she sent to the Swedish Academy. In the speech, titled "Sidelined," she asks, "what happens to those, who don't really know reality at all?"[27] As a writer, she goes on, she exists on the sidelines. On the one hand, she can see better from there — distance provides perspective. On the other hand, the true fullness of human life is beyond her grasp. Jelinek has always perceived herself to be several degrees of separation removed from reality. Only in recent years have her physical circumstances come to reflect this symbolic distance. Though her concerns encompass her native Austria's involvement in the Holocaust and its aftermath, the ravages of global capitalism, and the destruction of the environment, Jelinek's earliest works for the theater were focused on the subjugation of women and women's complicity in their own oppression. Throughout her career, this critique has been at the core of her work. Jelinek consistently takes the position that, since misogyny has from the beginning comprised the substrate of language itself, misogyny cannot be overcome without a new approach to language. According to Lacan, language is the domain of phallic exchange. Women do not have access to the symbolic order the way men do because "a woman [...] is not considered a subject."[28] Where a male writer can wield language as an instrument, a weapon, as a means of making direct contact with reality, and even as a means of shaping reality, women will always be operating within a discourse that was designed to exclude them. Women do not exchange; they are objects of exchange. "When a man speaks," Jelinek says, "he speaks

[27] Elfriede Jelinek, "Sidelined," lecture, Nobel Prize Summit at the Swedish Academy, Stockholm, Sweden, December 7, 2004, http://www.nobelprize.org/nobel_prizes/literature/laureates/2004/jelinek-lecture-e.html.

[28] Elfriede Jelinek, "I Am a *Trümmerfrau* of Language," *Theater* 36, no. 2 (2006): 27.

the discourse of authority. When a woman speaks, she does not. But what she can do is what I am doing, that is, to deal with this speechlessness, [...] if, as a woman, you don't have the right to speak, you've got to pick up the rubble. I am a *Trümmerfrau* of language."[29]

Here Jelinek identifies herself with the women who cleared out the rubble from bombed-out cities after World War II. Working with found materials, shattered, damaged materials, Honegger writes that "Jelinek's strategy of quoting is a form of ready-made speech acts taken from trashcans and the canon. [...] Jelinek does not discard anything from the garbage heap of words, which she spreads on her flat surfaces."[30] Following Bataille, creation is always already a process of waste management, managing one's own excess. For Jelinek, the woman writer self-conscious of her status as woman writer, writing is a matter of managing the waste of others. Already, as a woman, speaking in a foreign tongue, Jelinek finds herself doubly estranged by her social isolation. A self-confessed TV junkie, she relies on watching copious amounts of television for information about "reality." Everything is secondhand but also garishly buffed and polished, exaggerated, sped up, and underscored. Rather than making her less equipped to grapple with the complexities of the world she writes about, Jelinek's hypermediated existence lends itself to acute observation of the machinations of what is fast becoming our post-truth reality. Jelinek gives voice not to firsthand existential shame — existence is something she might say she has largely managed to avoid — but to the perspective of the horrified spectator.

Bambiland and the Society of the Spectacle

"When man's need for miracles is not satisfied," Bataille writes, "it transforms itself into a passion for destruction, being at cer-

---

29 Ibid., 29.
30 Gitta Honegger, "Introduction" to Elfriede Jelinek, *Rechnitz and The Merchant's Contracts* (New York: Seagull Books, 2015), 2.

tain moments the only possible miracle, preferable to boredom, be that as it may."³¹ War is the miracle humanity conjures for itself to hasten the erasure of its own excesses. War dazzles even as it decimates. "Such is the intensive employment of modern means of destruction: it is incontestable, prodigious, sensational," says Bataille.³²

The war that is the subject of Jelinek's 2003 play Bambiland is always already mediated, a war experienced via a screen even by many of those on the front lines, inflicting most of the casualties. The world of *Bambiland* takes place in what Baudrillard calls "the desert of the real," a place beyond "real" and "artificial," a place where representation precedes reality, where the map precedes the territory. Baudrillard died in 2007, before the extent of the US's covert drone strike program was revealed, but since the Gulf War he had often worried in print about "virtual warfare," war as spectacle, and the distancing, desensitizing effects of conducting a war that plays like a video game or action film.

"The politics of theatre is a *politics of perception*," Lehmann writes, "To define it we have to remember that the mode of perception in theatre cannot be separated from the existence of theatre in a world of media which massively shapes all perception."³³ In *Bambiland*, war is delivered to us in the form of an entertainment juggernaut of TV news images. Statistics, unattributed quotations, associations, digressions, puns, and pop culture detritus all run together in one long unbroken monologue. *Bambiland* has no designated characters and practically no stage directions. The play's excess and its intentional formlessness evoke the torrent of waste produced by advanced capitalism and the wars that must be fought to sustain it. The central recognizable figures of *Bambiland* are the architects of the Iraq War. Taking Aeschylus's *The Persians* as a (very) loose model, the play is nar-

---

31 Bataille, *The Cradle of Humanity*, 104.
32 Ibid.
33 Hans-Thies Lehmann, *Postdramatic Theatre*, trans. Karen Jürs-Munby (New York: Routledge, 2006), 185.

rated as though being watching on television by someone in a semi-comatose state as "the mighty Master of War," probably Cheney, is "marching his menfolk onward, [...] it's just part of our culture that we eventually get around to exercising a certain degree of force."[34] Jelinek depicts the conflict as "blood for oil" crusade fought by ignorant, pugnacious conquistador-cowboys on behalf of a nation of "clients. Consumers. Customer Kings."[35] The waste of oil is ironically treated as more of a calamity than the waste of a life. Compare:

> Where did all that oil go, unspent? Burning. Burning. Explosives set round the rigs where the oil wells up, where it goes up in flames and goes to waste. It's impossible to imagine, and hard to foresee. And anyone who might manage to spare himself from drowning in that tear-soaked sea of salt, the least we shall do is to kill him. You can set fire to our homes, set fire to our icons, just keep your fires off our oil and our television sets![36]

with:

> So many men laid to waste! What a waste — surely, I could have used the one or the other of them. My garden could have used one, or my walls, which need painting, could have used one of them too. And my bed sure could use something better than lonesome old me.[37]

The narrator/ventriloquist/viewer cannot empathize with the images on the screen for more than a few blinks before egocentric fantasies resume control. Lehmann argues that, however "true to life" the image conveyed by the high-speed contemporary media apparatus, "produced far from its reception and

---

34 Elfriede Jelinek, *Bambiland*, Theater 39, no. 3 (2009): 115.
35 Ibid., 125.
36 Ibid., 112.
37 Ibid., 124.

received far from its origin, it imprints indifference onto everything shown."[38] Fact and fiction alike are "dramatized" to the point where everything acquires an identical veneer of irreality. The graphics and audio effects used to turn presidential debates into rock-'em, sock-'em showdowns are identically to those used to punch up the World Series or Super Bowl.

An image is flat and unbreachable, textureless — one can purchase it but not get purchase on it. One is forced to consume it wholesale. This "seductive eyewash," as Jelinek puts it, anesthetizes viewers. However violent or ecstatic the imagery, it cannot rouse viewers from their coma of complacency.[39]

Rhetoric — language become image — can do the same. As Hannah Arendt writes, "Clichés, stock phrases, adherence to conventional, standardized codes of expression [...] have the socially recognized function of protecting us against reality."[40] In *Bambiland,* the true motivation behind the war is kept hidden behind an impenetrable wall of such rhetoric, which Jelinek parodies mercilessly:

> Look, people, the basic principle is that we are the only ones with any real principles: Ours is the only country where the individual counts anymore because every individual is an entity unto himself. [...] Every human individual counts. Every human individual counts his money. Some count more, others count less. Dick Cheney counts more, we count less.[41]

Jelinek catches American political discourse in its many hypocrisies and contradictions. "It only works when both are the same. But both people are different. This is the whole basis for our civilization — that people are different. It's just that those sand niggers don't see it that way," and periodically folds her own more straightforwardly caustic commentary in as well: "[w]ill you fi-

---

38 Lehmann, *Postdramatic Theatre,* 185.
39 Jelinek, *Bambiland,* 113.
40 Hannah Arendt, *The Life of the Mind* (New York: Harcourt, 1971), 4.
41 Ibid., 122.

nally deal a deathblow in the war against the alpha-male type as a model for humanity!"[42] For Jelinek, this model stands not just for violence, but for those narrowly capitalist values of "individualism" and "efficiency" that have motivated the US's frightening transformation from a democracy into a corporatocracy.

Bambiland stretches on like a discursive desert. There is no real sense of progress being made, of victory approaching, or even of sense gradually accreting. Voices that seem as though they cannot possibly be human praise self-targeting smart-bombs and "advanced surveillance systems that take the human eye out of the act of seeing."[43] The "climax" comes near the end of the play when God Himself makes an appearance. Rather than pass judgment or issue a command, He promptly commences with fellating an American warhead. While narrating this experience, He reaffirms the American mandate, unconvincingly explains that "our side" is justified in killing thousands of people, including civilians, with imprecise, hyper-destructive cluster bombs because doing so enables us "to keep our losses at an absolute minimum."[44] God wonders "whether we'll ever be satisfied," though it is not clear whether He is thinking of the greed of Americans or of His fellatee and the threat of lockjaw.[45] The capitalist, by definition, can never be satisfied — growth demands constant escalation — and the capitalist, by definition, must count only her own losses before considering those of the enemy. *Bambiland* presciently anticipates Donald Trump's "America First" style of nationalism and commitment to running the country "like a business," where generating profits for a handful of top shareholders takes precedence over any other mission. The military-industrial complex is the only real "winner" in *Bambiland*, forcing even God and Country to submit. The play ends when God's hoplophilic blowjob does: "Finally,

---

42 Ibid.
43 Colin Mannex, "Preface to Elfriede Jelinek's *Bambiland*," *Theater* 39, no. 3 (2009): 107.
44 Jelinek, *Bambiland*, 140.
45 Ibid.

he shoots his wad. I thought he was never going to come," Our Father says. "So. Now that's the end of that."[46]

Rechnitz and the Exterminating Angel of History

The Persians, *Bambiland*'s chief dramatic intertext, is considered to be the oldest surviving play in the history of theater. Like *Bambiland*, it is a history play. As Aeschylus did in writing *The Persians*, with *Bambiland* Jelinek was chronicling history practically in real time, dealing with current events as they were still unfolding, but she frequently makes a point of revisiting closed cases, digging up buried histories, especially contentious ones. Generally, history is written by the victors, but Jelinek is committed to (re)writing history from the perspective of the vanquished, from the perspective of those whose voices and even traces have been erased from the official record.

The relationship of Jelinek's Austria to the ascent of the Nazis before the Second World War is part of a particularly contentious national history. After the war, while Germany itself was carved up into externally administered segments and forced to undergo an extensive "de-Nazification" process, Austria was able to downplay their complicity and contributions to the Holocaust by claiming that they were merely Hitler's first victims, the targets of the aggressive foreign policy of the Nazis. This was a convenient fiction, now referred to as the "victim myth" (*Opfermythos*). In fact, when Hitler marched into Vienna after the 1938 annexation (*Anschluß*) of Austria, he was greeted with a parade. Austria has never entirely let go of the victim myth, which began to give way to a more accurate picture of the period between 1938 and 1945 only after many years and tremendous international pressure. Not until 1998 did Austria even appoint a committee to begin addressing questions of restitution dating from the war years.

Jelinek's *Rechnitz* confronts the gaps in official historical narratives by focusing on one macabre evening in a small Austri-

---

46 Ibid., 143.

an town on the Hungarian border in 1945. Rechnitz castle was owned by Count and Countess Bátthyany and served as a residence for local Nazi leaders during the war. On March 24, 1945 the Countess threw a lavish party. In attendance was Rechnitz's Gestapo chief, Franz Podezin, who was also rumored to be the Countess's lover at the time. During the party, Podezin received orders to pick up 200 Jewish inmates deemed too sick or weak to work who were being transported to Rechnitz by train from a nearby forced labor camp in Kőszeg. They were put up at the castle's stables and shot by party guests, to whom guns had been distributed during the festivities. To this day, the site of the mass grave has not been found.[47] The case has been a highly controversial issue in Austria ever since. Residents of Rechnitz boycotted the investigation. In 1946 a witness was murdered and "other witnesses died in mysterious accidents."[48]

Jelinek's play is subtitled "The Exterminating Angel," a reference to Luis Buñuel's 1962 film of that title. In Buñuel's film, a dinner party held at a mansion for an upper crust group turns darkly surreal when at the end of the evening the guests find themselves unable to leave the music room to which they have retired for some after-dinner entertainment. There are no physical barriers preventing them from leaving, but despite hunger, serious illness, and crushing despair, the power of some collective hallucination keeps them trapped in the room for many weeks. The spell is only broken when, by some chance, the group finds themselves arranged in precisely the same physical configuration they were in on the evening of the party. Repetition and remembrance set them free, though there are casualties; some of their number do not make it out of the mansion alive.

Jelinek portrays the elite group turning mass murder into a party game that night in the Rechnitz castle as suffering from a collective hallucination by denial of their own, a collective hal-

---

47 Honegger, "Introduction," 6.
48 "Mass Murder as Party Entertainment?" *Der Spiegel*, October 22, 2007, https://www.spiegel.de/international/germany/historians-dispute-journalist-s-claims-mass-murder-as-party-entertainment-a-512869.html.

lucination that has never been dispelled because remembrance continues to be forestalled. Jelinek has described the process of writing *Rechnitz* as an attempt to "write a play around a blind spot."[49] To do this, she assembles a chorus of messengers, who offer competing descriptions of that fateful evening of March 24 as well as competing philosophies of truth and the transmission of traumatic memory.

In classical Attic tragedy, from which Jelinek habitually borrows characters, scenarios, conventions, and motifs, the voice of the messenger is one we trust implicitly. The dramatis personae and the audience rely on messengers to convey in language what is not representable in images. In *Rechnitz*, the accounts of the messenger(s) are continuously interrupted with slippery qualifications that undermine confidence in their veracity: "I tell it how it is, I tell you what I was told, literally."[50] Which is it? "I saw it with my own eyes, at least I think they were my own."[51] No eyewitness seems to trust their own perceptions. Eventually the chain of information becomes so vexed that it can no longer be said with any certainty that there were any eyewitnesses present at the event in question at all. Everyone wants to disavow responsibility:

> [S]he started to shoot, the countess, the reports contradict one another already, what's going to happen next, and most importantly, to whom? And she kept shooting, the countess, bang, bang, she shot them down, and she shot and shot, or did she not shoot at all? Did she just shoot off from the castle? And we confused it with her usual freewheeling antics and our far-fetched semantics (remember now, we weren't there).[52]

---

49 Elfriede Jelinek, quoted in Honegger, "Introduction," 11.
50 Jelinek, *Rechnitz and The Merchant's Contracts*, 94.
51 Ibid., 143.
52 Ibid., 130.

If all of history is reduced to semantic gymnastics, the guilty can never be brought to justice. The undead appear frequently throughout Jelinek's oeuvre, a continuing reminder that the dead cannot rest in peace until the truth about their murderers is known. For Jelinek, the combination of Austria's disinclination to acknowledge its sordid past and the global drift towards a post-truth media landscape accelerated by technology portends disaster. Like Buñuel's well-coiffed society types who descend into savagery and derangement when trapped in the echo chamber of their mutually-reinforcing delusions, the messengers of *Rechnitz* have lost the ability to think for themselves. They have conceded their right to move, shape, and write history — history, rather, moves them, as Fukuyama imagined it would. As Jelinek puts it in one passage, they have their heads up history's ass:

> [T]his story can't be true, says the historian, who did a colonoscopy on history from the other end as it were, but it stayed dark […], makes no difference anyway, he would have seen only darkness from any direction. He wouldn't see a thing, even if it were shown to him in a picture, because he is used to finding out everything from pictures.[53]

A generation raised on finding everything out from pictures stands even less of a chance of being able to read between the lines of official histories, those written by the victorious, the powerful, those who can afford to buy the truth:

> In every proper history the wealthy, the stuffed man, the stuffed-up man has his representative, who handles all his stuff and takes care of his shit, I mean he has to take care of all the shit in place of his master. History only tunes its instruments, but it rarely gets to play. Life is very long. But today is one of those days history is playing with us as if life would never end. We are its instruments. We are in tune. We

53 Ibid., 70.

> bring history in tune with us. Our testimonies must hit the right tone and we should all sing to the same tune. No, we never get it right and no one listens to us anyway. So the story should be looked at in peace and quiet"[54]

When Lehmann describes the ways in which contemporary mass media severs actor from action and speaker from speech, he could well be describing the dramaturgical mechanism of *Rechnitz*: "[w]e have the impression that individuals are reporting to us, but in fact it is collectives, who for their part represent nothing but *functions of the medium*." [55] Their language speaks them. No one is an originator. No one owns truth or meaning. Everyone is only a messenger, not responsible for or intimately associated with the content of what they have to deliver. "On the one hand," Lehmann observes, "the medium releases the senders from all connection with the emitted message and, on the other hand, it occults the viewers' perception of the fact that participation in language also makes them, the receivers, responsible for the message."[56]

Jelinek presents questions of historical fact and responsibility as irretrievably "occulted" in *Rechnitz*. Rather than doing the necessary work of sifting through the layers of obfuscation and deception that have accumulated over the years since the Rechnitz massacre and other wartime atrocities, she sees countries with Nazi pasts doubling down on tried and true strategies for misdirection, once again looking for scapegoats in the form of outsiders, immigrants, and refugees. Grimacing at the image of Austria exported to attract tourism — idyllic, Alpine, dirndled in *The Sound of Music* style — she strikes at the violence undergirding this Hollywood stereotype. "I am sure you want to know more about the so-called Europa Warranty," a speaker ventriloquizing a travel agent says, "which we added to your package, so you won't be scared — it guarantees that Europe's hot springs

---

54 Ibid.
55 Lehmann, *Postdramatic Theatre*, 185.
56 Ibid.

function free of harmful germs of foreigners, but only if no foreigners are let in."[57] Tourism comprises nearly nine percent of Austria's gross domestic product, and if the truth is bad for business, there will always be ways of massaging that truth into something that will look better on the brochure.

Planned Obsolescence: Death of a Salesman

The US emerged from the Second World War without the Teutonic burden of "too much memory."[58] The experience of saving the world from the scourge of fascism left Americans with a Bambi-esque belief in their country's innocence and righteousness. The belief that America is an unequivocal force for good in the world has long motivated our foreign policy. The idea that the world needs our intervention if global order is to be maintained has made it easier for the public to accept the death tolls. In the post-WWII period when the US was experiencing a period of unprecedented economic prosperity, this faith in American exceptionalism was at its apogee, but Arthur Miller turned his attention to those the American dream had left behind in his 1949 *Death of a Salesman*. Affluence is a form of potential energy and, as Bataille observes, "excess energy provides for the growth or the turbulence of individuals."[59] While, socially and politically, Americans were focused on growth, Miller saw turbulence.

The motif of waste is dominant throughout *Death of a Salesman*. Willy Loman is plagued by planned obsolescence, a recent capitalist invention that ensures that everything from the refrigerator to the car is constantly breaking down and needing to be replaced. Willy's frustration with this type of systemic wastefulness has to do not with "excess" desire — waste as the product of effort over-spilling the capacity of consumption — but with

---

57 Jelinek, *Rechnitz and The Merchant's Contracts*, 88.
58 Schlipphacke, *Nostalgia after Nazism*, 75.
59 Georges Bataille, *The Accursed Share*, trans. Robert Hurley (New York: Zone Books, 1991), 1:128.

material waste and the enervating perpetual maintenance work it requires. Willy is just barely able to keep his house from falling down around his ears, but he is not in forward motion. He is not advancing professionally, financially, or personally. He has a passionate and volatile relationship with the *stuff* his dwindling commission enables him to buy, and he contradicts himself constantly, sometimes within the space of a few lines, never apparently noticing a pattern. At first, his new Chevrolet is "the greatest car ever built."[60] Just a few years later, Willy is railing, "that goddam Chevrolet, they ought to prohibit the manufacture of that car."[61]

Nevertheless, the Lomans persist in their belief in in the integrity of advertising. When Willy fumes about their brand-new refrigerator needing repairs, Linda soothes him by reminding him that the company that manufactures it has "got the biggest ads." "I know," he says, somehow reassured, "it's a fine machine."[62] An advertisement works, when it works, by creating anxieties that it promises can be assuaged simply by purchasing a particular product. It generates new wants, and if it succeeds in convincing the consumer that those wants are needs, the advertisement is a success. In a post-*Mad Men* era, the Lomans's faith in the institution of advertising seems comically naive, but the transformations the advertising industry underwent during the 1940s had thoroughly conditioned Americans to be so trusting.

Because the business of advertising absorbs resources without producing anything strictly *necessary,* in times of scarcity advertising budgets once presented an obvious opportunity for trimming the fat. This was the case during the First World War, when many manufacturers reoriented their operations in order to produce war materials instead of consumer goods and backed off of advertising nonessential products for the duration of the

---

60 Arthur Miller, *Death of a Salesman* (New York: Dramatists Play Service, 1948), 23.
61 Ibid., 25.
62 Ibid.

crisis. Things changed, however, during the Second World War when US companies *increased* spending on advertising from $2.1 billion in 1941 to $2.8 billion in 1945.[63] Even companies who couldn't afford to meet pre-war levels of demand due to the diversion of crucial resources invested heavily in advertising to keep their products tantalizingly alive in the minds of their past and future customer bases. When they didn't have anything to sell, corporations ran ads encouraging Americans to buy war bonds — flaunting one's patriotism was good for business, too. The government itself got into advertising in a way that blurred the lines between public service announcement, propaganda, entertainment, and private profit. The corporate *brand* was well on its way to attaining the status of quasi-religious icon that it now enjoys. "Think of the brand," Naomi Klein writes, "as the core meaning of the modern corporation, and of the advertisement as one vehicle used to convey that meaning to the world"[64] As the corporation takes its place at the center of American public life, the human inclination towards wastefulness is suppressed, and the principle of producing at the least expense becomes the "meaning" not only of the corporation, but of our individual lives as well.

The more successful a company is at insinuating itself into the public consciousness as humane (Google's motto: "Don't be evil.") or at least human-centered (Facebook's stated goal of connecting the world), the better it often is at diverting power away from actual humans. The insidious rise of the ostensibly benevolent corporation began in earnest during the *Death of a Salesman* era. In the 1940s, for example, the then-behemoth-in-the-making Walt Disney Company had yet to establish itself as an effective synonym for family-friendly Americana, but it was already working with the government to produce training and propaganda films for the US Army and Navy. Some were dry,

---

63 "1940s War, Cold War and Consumerism," *Advertising Age*, March 28, 2005, http://adage.com/article/75-years-of-ideas/1940s-war-cold-war-consumerism/102702/.

64 Naomi Klein, *No Logo: Taking Aim at Brand Bullies* (New York: Picador, 2000), 5.

technical affairs initially shown only to audiences of servicemen, but some were widely distributed zany romps trafficking in crowd-pleasing racial stereotypes featuring beloved cartoon characters like Donald Duck holding his own against the Nazi's (1943's "Der Fuehrer's Face," "Education for Death") or the Japanese (1944's "Commando Duck"). In one ingenious example of Disney's exploiting the inroads it had already made into the psyche of the average American, the company repurposed the distinctive actor Fred Shields, who had voiced the character of the supremely authoritative "Great Prince of the Forest" in 1942's *Bambi,* deploying him as a narrator in a cartoon short called "The Spirit of '43" exhorting Americans to pay their taxes.[65] These tax dollars, Bambi's father told the nation, would fund the crucial manufacturing of "machine guns, anti-tank guns, long-range guns, guns, guns, all kinds of guns!" Every dollar spent for something you didn't need rather than saved to "pay your taxes" was, catchily, "a dollar to help the Axis." Serving as the US government's cuddliest propagandist lent the company a kind of gravitas that would have been difficult to acquire had they remained strictly purveyors of entertainment.

Disney was not above pressing its mice into service for lesser goods, too. A 1939 animated short called "Mickey's Surprise Party" is perceptually indistinguishable from any other Disney cartoon of the era until the last thirty seconds or so, when it is revealed to be a commercial. The short opens with Minnie Mouse in full, aproned, domestic splendor, chirping as she mixes up a bowl of dough, "[w]e're gonna surprise Mickey with some cookies like his mother used to make." But alas, it is not to be. By the time an amorous and hungry Mickey arrives, a series of disasters in the kitchen have rendered the cookies inedible. Minnie collapses into operatic sobs, wailing, "I wanted to make those cookies like your mother used to make, and now they're all burnt up!" To console her, Mickey laughs, "[o]h, my mother used to burn 'em all the time." The little lady is inconsolable.

---

65 J.D. Connor, lecture in the course "The Art of Disney," Yale University, New Haven, Fall, 2015.

Still intent on salvaging their romantic date, Mickey dashes out to the store and returns with a box of Nabisco™ products. "Oh, Mickey! Nabisco! Lorna Doone! Social Teas! And Oreos!" she coos, each product arousing her more than the last. "Yeah, my mother used to buy 'em all the time," Mickey says. Reassured that a simple trip to the supermarket can elevate her to the status of primary love object in her beau's eyes, Minnie covers Mickey in kisses. Nabisco products cure Oedipal anxieties and leave young couples with more free time for canoodling.

The fact that "The Spirit of '43" and "Mickey's Surprise Party" were both very recognizably Walt Disney productions reflects the burgeoning importance of the brand as icon, in the devotional sense. Indeed, the words we most frequently see associated with the word brand itself are "trust," "loyalty," and "faith." "Disney invented the game" of modern branding, Klein writes, but spawned a host of imitators, all of whom hoped to inspire in consumers a fervor once reserved for things like religious faith or patriotism.[66] *Death of a Salesman* was written at a moment when the place of religion in the American public consciousness was undergoing an important transformation. Before the Second World War, with the country mired in the Great Depression, religious movements such as the Social Gospel, which took direct aim at economic inequality and other capitalist ills, experienced a resurgence. After the war, Christianity was rebranded as inherently capitalist and enlisted in the struggle against "godless communism." Religion became patriotic and capitalism became religious. Like other objects of religious devotion, a corporate brand stood for something. Brands are supposed to encapsulate and communicate *values*. Americans have perhaps never been as trusting, faithful, and loyal to their country as they were in the *Death of a Salesman* era. With the war won, the bounty of a robust economy, and the comforts of hearth and home waiting to be enjoyed, a sense of optimism, even invincibility, was practically compulsory. What more could they possibly want? In this exceptional country peopled by heroes and

---

66 Klein, *No Logo*, 156.

innocents, the notion that the economy is rigged, that there exist among us malevolent forces and individuals who do not have the interests of the majority at heart was not a fashionable idea. More likely, if hardship struck or a flicker of doubt troubled an otherwise peaceful mind, one was more likely to look inside the self for the source of the failure, to commit to playing the rigged game harder, better.

Miller pointedly does not specify what it is that Willy sells, but he likely attempts to do unto others just what those misleading advertisements do to him. The functions of advertising and salesmanship are the same; both consist of pushing products that people do not really need, products that will soon be garbage. One of Willy's many blind spots prevents him from seeing that he is perpetuating the same capitalist swindle that leaves him feeling as though he's desperately running from month to month just to stay in the same place. Of course, the most difficult lesson for Willy to learn is that under capitalism, he himself will ultimately be reduced to the status of waste and discarded. When he ceases to be productive, he is unceremoniously fired. "You can't eat the orange and throw the peel away," he implores his boss Howard.[67] But of course you can. And of course Howard does.

Phallic Coprophilia: Norman Mailer's <u>Ancient Evenings</u> and Matthew Barney's <u>River of Fundament</u>

Over half a century later, American exceptionalism having taken some hard knocks, the sculptor Matthew Barney seized on waste as a symbol of rebirth and regeneration for his 2014 symphonic film, *River of Fundament,* in which, as one critic put it, "[w]estern civilization's foundation is also humanity's anus."[68] A five hour opera scored by Jonathan Bepler, the project has also

---

67 Miller, *Death of a Salesman,* 59.
68 Christopher Knight, "Matthew Barney's 'River of Fundament'? Well, It's Certainly Big," *Los Angeles Times,* September 26, 2015, https://www.latimes.com/entertainment/arts/museums/la-ca-cm-knight-barney-review-20150927-column.html.

been shared with the public in the form of exhibitions of objects made for the film and during the filmmaking process, a way of foregrounding the residue of the film, giving its own waste products an afterlife. Shot in New York, Los Angeles, and in the contemporary wasteland of Detroit, where the decline of the American automobile industry becomes both Barney's central subject and metaphor for American masculinity (or America as masculinity): the possibilities of the open road, speed, power, mobility, the virile wonder of heavy machinery transforming base metals into a muscle car. The film is earnestly worshipful of these things, never connecting them to, for example, the unsustainable levels of pollution generated by car culture. For Barney, waste is infinitely fecund. If life is woman's gift to the world, waste is man's. While aggression is everywhere in *River of Fundament,* the world Barney renders is not consumed by a war of all against all; homoerotic violence is elevated to the level of religious ritual, giving form and meaning to all social life.

While the film's libretto borrows from Walt Whitman, its principal source is Norman Mailer's *Ancient Evenings.* The novel is a narration of narration, a story of stories being told over the course of a long dinner in Ancient Egypt, and narrative coherence is not one of the film's priorities — visual coherence is. Early in the film, the penis and the turd are symbolically conflated, with each precious package depicted wrapped in gold foil. Barney spatially transposes Mailer's story but does not make a clean temporal break. Ancient mythology and iterations of archaic deities are very much present in Barney's contemporary America, beginning with a wake for Mailer shot in a replica of the dead author's apartment. Supra- and supernatural characters from the novel arrive drenched in shit to mingle with what's left of the late-twentieth century quintessentially New York culturati — Fran Lebowitz, Elaine Stritch, real-life writers, artists, and musicians playing themselves. They burst into song at irregular intervals as guests dine on maggot-infested hors d'oeuvres made from produce fertilized by the Pharoah's feces and discuss Mailer's legacy. Barney originally conceived of the piece as a work for the stage, and indeed, it can be seen as a piece of postdramatic theater, with Mailer's text serving as a reservoir of images upon which to draw in order to create something that ultimately far surpasses its source material.[69]

Kate Millett characterized Mailer as "a prisoner of the virility cult" and as a man whose "powerful intellectual comprehension of what is most dangerous in the masculine sensibility is exceeded only by his attachment to the malaise."[70] This critique is not immediately discernible in the visual discourse of *River of Fundament* and in the conversations that float around the two sarcophagi occupying prominent places in Mailer's library during the depicted wake: "[t]hat's one of the greatest innovations of Normal Mailer, proclaiming his own brilliance," someone says. *Ancient Evenings* is a novel about sodomy and coprophagy, life and death. Menenhetet I, obsessed with immortality, manages to secure his own infinite insistence by mystically climbing into the womb of a lover during sex in order to be reborn. Barney's film finds a grotesque analogue in having a young "Norman" slit open the belly of a dead, bloated cow and bury himself inside, closing the first act of the three-part film. Norman will achieve two rebirths but fail a third time. Woman, the Feminine, is positioned in both Mailer's and Barney's projects as vessel and inanimate object, but perhaps more productively as the "piss and shit" between which we are all born.[71]

The Feminine is irrelevant in Mailer's universe unless it exists to serve as a passageway to eternity or a novel tourist destination for men being sodomized and through this experience becoming acquainted with their own submissive homosexual desires. After hundreds of pages of hyper-macho, orgiastic fighting and fucking, the first detailed description of a vagina is treated as an obscenity, something Menenhetet only feels comfortable speaking of since "the boy," our narrator, is presumed to be asleep.[72]

---

69 Matthew Barney, Q&A session following screening of *River of Fundament*, IFC Center, New York, December 6, 2015.
70 Kate Millet, *Sexual Politics* (New York: Columbia University Press, 1969), 314.
71 Norman Mailer, *Ancient Evenings* (Boston: Little Brown, 1983), 69.
72 Ibid., 307.

The anus, however, is treated with a kind of transcendent, universal reverence. Menenhetet tells us that:

> In Khert-Neter, there is a river of feces deep as a pit. Across it, the dead must swim. The Ka of all but the wisest, most prepared, or the most courageous, will expire in that river, weeping for their mother. They have forgotten how they came out of her. Between piss and shit are we born, and in water do we die the first time, slipping off to death on the release of our waters. [...] [S]hame and waste may be buried in shit, but so is many a rich and tender sentiment as well. [...] How then can this cauldron of emotion be no more than a burial chamber? Is it not also part of the womb of all that is yet to come? Is not part of time reborn, by necessity, in shit? Where else can be found those unresolved passions which — frustrated, unworked, maniacal — must now labor twice as hard to germinate the future?[73]

John Scanlan defines waste as "dead matter."[74] For Mailer's ancient Egyptians, death is not the full stop that it is for modern mortals, and thus they are able to see more clearly the power of this "dead matter." It is by dining on bat feces that Menenhetet (or "Norman" in Barney's film) learns how to recycle his soul — by recycling lover into mother. "Excrement is full of all that is too despicable for us, but it also may contain all that we cannot afford to take into ourselves — all that is too rich, too courageous, or too proud for our bearing."[75] Bataille holds ancient Egypt up as the pinnacle of what he calls "societies of consumption" as distinguished from societies of acquisition. Where today we are spiritually miserly, meager, the Ancient Egyptians were capable of building the pyramid, most prodigious and prodigal of tombs. Bataille and Mailer would have us see in such glorious extravagance possibilities attainable even by those of us whose

---

73 Ibid., 69–70.
74 John Scanlan, *On Garbage* (London: Reaktion Books, 2005), 115.
75 Mailer, *Ancient Evenings*, 207.

relationship to death and time does not include the existence of an afterlife. For the Ancient Egyptians, it seems, we cannot, or do not use up our various potentials in a single lifetime — our bounty is as boundless as the sea. For modern humans, it seems we never have enough; people die full of regret, having fallen short, having lost the race, having failed to recoup, filled with bitterness that the world didn't deliver all that it once promised. In taking death as merely a light suggestion, Mailer's characters are less inclined to save themselves; potentially infinite chances lie before them, at least for the men.

Mailer flips conventional models of time that associate the masculine with linearity and the feminine with cyclicality — the narrator's mother Hathfertiti interjects at one point that "[w]omen search for the bottom of their grief. If they can find it, they are ready for another man. Why, if I were ever to weep for a lover and learn that my sorrow was bottomless, I would know he was the man I must follow into the Land of the Dead."[76] This idea of terminal grief is also a vision of excess, but shows woman revealed to herself not in infinitely repeatable acts of love or war, but in bereavement. Man is born to lay waste. Woman is born to lose.

River of Fundament builds to an epic struggle between two "gods" vying for rule. A contemporary stand-in for Horus tricks a version of Set into eating Horus's semen, after which a battle is staged in a dry dock at the Brooklyn Navy Yard, with hundreds of spectators looking on. The film's parallel narrative, following the reincarnations of the iconic American automobile, culminates here, too. We begin with the 1967 Chrysler Crown Imperial, a car Barney chose because of its reputation for being virtually indestructible. The Chrysler is transformed into a 1979 Pontiac Firebird Trans Am, the last, best, example of the original muscle-car generation. At the end of the battle between Horus and Seth, the car is reborn again as a 2001 Ford Crown Victoria Police Interceptor, the vehicle of choice for twenty-first-century American police cruisers. This last iteration evokes the repres-

76 Ibid., 348.

sive power of the state, not the uninhibited machismo of the cowboy, and it mirrors Norman's inability to survive into a third self. War between equals gives way to state-sponsored violence. The scale shifts, and the individual will is subsumed by the collective. These transfigurations and failed transfigurations reveal a self-destructive undercurrent to an apparently megalomaniacal strain of American virility. The desire to dominate becomes the desire to obliterate the self in mutual conflagration.

3

Crisis of Imagination: The Anthropocene

> *The anthropocentric sense of life has been shaken.*
> *[…] There is a universal feeling, a universal fear, that*
> *our progress in controlling nature may increasingly*
> *help to weave that very calamity it is supposed to*
> *protect us from, that it may be weaving that second*
> *nature into which society has rankly grown.*
> — Theodor Adorno, *Negative Dialectics*[1]

With the advance of globalization, the question of where and how the US and other developed nations dispose of their waste has become increasingly vexed. Centuries of colonial and neocolonial exploitation have left much of the developing world politically, economically, and infrastructurally crippled. It has also become clear that these same developing nations will bear the early brunt of the detrimental effects of climate change brought about by the more developed nations' unrestrained greenhouse gas emissions during the nineteenth and twentieth centuries. Impoverished African countries are the most vulnerable to devastating droughts and low-lying, coastal, Southeast Asian countries to floods. We have entered what many scientists have come

---

1 Theodor Adorno, *Negative Dialectics*, trans. E.B. Ashton (New York: The Continuum Publishing Company, 1973), 67.

to refer to as the "Anthropocene," the proposed designation for the present geological epoch, one in which human activity has made the most lasting impact on the changing planet, acidifying the ocean, altering the atmosphere, and bringing about mass extinctions of plant and animal species.[2] In 2018 the United Nations' Intergovernmental Panel on Climate Change issued a report describing the disastrous effects of allowing the atmosphere to warm just 1.5 degrees Celsius above pre-industrial levels by 2040, as we are currently on track to do: food shortages, the dispersal of invasive species, the loss of biodiversity, melting polar icecaps, rising sea levels, the spread of disease, and an increase in catastrophic isolated extreme weather events.[3] In essence, for a child born today, the world will likely have been consumed by fire, flood, and tempest by the time she comes of age. According to the UN report, we can avoid such an outcome only by totally and immediately transforming the world's economy. Even once coal power is eliminated, existing emissions will linger in the atmosphere and continue to cause damage for years.

It is all but inconceivable that we will transform the world's economy quickly enough. Any hope we had evaporated with the election of Donald Trump, who has said that the notion of climate change is a hoax perpetrated by the Chinese to make US manufacturing less competitive.[4] The US has contributed more than any other country to the atmospheric carbon dioxide that is responsible for rising temperatures, but in 2017, Trump announced his intention to withdraw the US from the Paris Agreement on climate change, "absent the identification of terms that are more favorable to the American people."[5] He has devoted

2   Paul J. Crutzen, "Geology of Mankind," *Nature* 415 (2000): art. 23.
3   IPCC, "Summary for Policymakers," in *Global Warming of 1.5°C*, https://www.ipcc.ch/sr15/chapter/spm/.
4   @realDonaldTrump (Donald J. Trump), *Twitter*, November 6, 2012, 2:15pm, https://twitter.com/realDonaldTrump/status/265895292191248385; *Twitter*, January 29, 2014, 1:27am, https://twitter.com/realDonaldTrump/status/428414113463955457.
5   Jane A. Leggett, "Potential Implications of U.S. Withdrawal from the Paris Agreement on Climate Change," *Congressional Research Service*, April 5, 2019, https://crsreports.congress.gov/product/pdf/IF/IF10668.

his presidency to eviscerating regulations designed to promote conservation domestically and frequently promises that his administration will "bring back coal." During the G7 summit in August 2019, as the Amazon rainforest burned, Trump declined to even make himself available for a meeting on climate change attended by the other six world leaders present.

In his book *The Great Derangement: Climate Change and the Unthinkable,* Amitav Ghosh argues that the impending climate catastrophe represents not so much a crisis of nature as a crisis of culture. Climate change poses a problem so enormous that the human imagination is confounded by it, with few artists able to address its consequences or imagine possible alternatives to our current suicide run. It is a reality that only becomes real when it is too late, when one's home is already underwater. The government of Maldives, whose 350,000 inhabitants live on a collection of coral islands an average of just 2.1 meters above sea level, staged one of the most powerful performance art pieces about climate change to date when in 2009, cabinet members in scuba gear held a meeting underwater to sign a document calling on all countries to cut their emissions in preparation for a UN climate change conference in Copenhagen. Their plea read:

> We must unite in a world war effort to halt further temperature rises. Climate change is happening and it threatens the rights and security of everyone on Earth. We have to have a better deal. We should be able to come out with an amicable understanding that everyone survives. If Maldives can't be saved today, we do not feel that there is much of a chance for the rest of the world.[6]

The imbalance between those nations responsible for *producing* the bulk of the waste and the nations now struggling most

---

6 "Maldives Government Highlights the Impact of Climate Change — By Meeting Underwater," *Daily Mail,* October 20, 2009, http://www.dailymail.co.uk/news/article-1221021/Maldives-underwater-cabinet-meeting-held-highlight-impact-climate-change.html.

desperately with its disposal was, perhaps inadvertently, underscored by *Holoscenes,* an ambitious project that Lars Jan's company Early Morning Opera installed in Times Square in June 2017 as a part of the World Science Festival. Without explicitly citing it as an influence, *Holoscenes* echoed the aesthetics of the Maldives cabinet meeting/performance at considerably greater expense. The performance took place inside a twelve-ton aquarium in the middle of the pulsing heart of the consumerist West (it costs companies millions of dollars monthly to rent advertising space on some of Times Square's larger LED screens). A rotating cast of individual performers entered the empty aquarium and began going about some piece of daily business such as reading a newspaper, making the bed, or tuning a guitar. Then a powerful custom hydraulic system would gradually flood the aquarium and the performers would struggle to complete their tasks as the water rose above their heads.

The title *Holoscenes* puns on the warped, slice-of-life vignettes presented by the performers in shifts and the Holocene, the geological epoch. According to the International Commission on Stratigraphy, the body of geologists charged with determining the absolute ages of the earth's rock layers, the Holocene began approximately 11,700 years ago and encompasses the entire history of human civilization up to and including the present. Other scientists believe that the Holocene has come to an end, and the philosopher Timothy Morton has suggested that the Anthropocene began with the invention of the steam engine in 1784.[7] The stated aim of Jan's project was to offer "an elemental portrait of our collective myopia, persistence, and for both better and worse, adaptation" in the face of climate change.[8] While the piece successfully conjured a vision of a future that might find wealthy New Yorkers inconvenienced by a soggy morning *Times,* it failed to take into account the irony of concocting

---

7   Timothy Morton, *Hyperobjects: Philosophy and Ecology after the End of the World* (Minneapolis: University of Minnesota Press, 2013), 4.
8   "Holoscenes," *The Times Square Arts,* http://www.timessquarenyc.org/times-square-arts/projects/at-the-crossroads/holoscenes/index.aspx.

such an extravagantly wasteful ecologically-minded spectacle. In terms of environmental and aesthetic impact, the Maldives cabinet's performance is clearly superior, even if they lacked the resources to put together a production on the scale of Jan's.

This imbalance is not accidental. When Lawrence Summers was vice president of the World Bank, he wrote a memo suggesting that since many countries in the less-developed world "are vastly under-polluted," wealthy nations such as the US could afford to pay poor countries to accept toxic waste products that we would prefer not to have decomposing in our own backyards.[9] While the unequally distributed effects of pollution almost certainly pose the greatest long-term challenges for the planet, other forms of global inequality are not merely a thing of the future. Sixty-million tons of food (approximately $162 billion worth) are wasted each year in the United States.[10] One-third of all the food produced in the world is never consumed. This wasted food would be more than sufficient to feed all of the world's 870 million hungry people.

Chekhov and His Discontents

Anton Chekhov's 1898 *Uncle Vanya* marks the beginning of Western theater artists' attention to issues of ecology. Chekhov's plays are also early exemplars of a dramaturgy of waste in that so much of what is of interest transpires in what goes unspoken, missed, squandered. There is often a kind of hole in Chekhov's dramaturgy: dramatic activity is organized around non-events rather than events. *The Cherry Orchard*'s Lopakhin never proposes to Varya. *The Three Sisters'* Prozorov women never make it to Moscow. The thematic tug of war between love and work, *eros*

9   Michael Perelman, *Transcending the Economy: On the Potential of Passionate Labor and the Wastes of the Market* (New York: Palgrave, 2000), 7.
10 Ron Nixon, "Food Waste Is Becoming Serious Economic and Environmental Issue, Report Says," *New York Times,* February 25, 2015, https://www.nytimes.com/2015/02/26/us/food-waste-is-becoming-serious-economic-and-environmental-issue-report-says.html.

and civilization, is the crux of Chekhov. Here, the latter is always reached for as a kind of palliative for the former. This *agōn* between pain and boredom, loneliness and disgust, is always present. Where love (or the dream of it) is, like life, fleeting, work is, like death, permanent. Love flourishes only at the expense of work. Because work must eventually resume, love must end.

All dreams suffer a similar fate in Chekhov. While issues of ecological waste and climate destruction are not the central concern, they loom over several of the plays, foreshadowing the havoc soon to be visited on a world privileging short-sighted, unsustainable rates of growth, productivity, and consumption. In *Uncle Vanya*, Astrov is a doctor who tends to the ailments of his fellow human beings, people whose pain can only be alleviated temporarily. He also thinks about longer-term interventions into the suffering of the world. In his spare time, Astrov maps the countryside, comparing the footprint of the forests in successive generations and noting with concern the effects of deforestation and other manmade affronts to nature. He is a vegetarian. He plants trees. He is an early environmentalist with an alarmingly prescient outlook on the trajectory of human life on earth:

> All our great woodlands are being leveled, millions of trees already gone, bird and animal habitats destroyed, rivers damned up and polluted—and all for what? Because we're too lazy to look for other sources of energy! […] You have to be a barbarian to burn all that beauty in your stove, to destroy something that can never be replaced. We were born with the ability to reason and the power to create and be fruitful, but until now all we've done is destroy whatever we see. The forests are disappearing one by one, the rivers are polluted, wildlife is becoming extinct, the climate is changing for the worse, every day the planet gets poorer and uglier. It's a disaster![11]

11 Anton Chekhov, *Uncle Vanya*, in *The Plays of Anton Chekhov*, trans. Paul Schmidt (New York: HarperCollins, 1997), 217.

An overemphasis on productivity and short-term profit lay waste to the unquantifiable. Astrov embodies the best ideals of *homo faber*. His conservation work is intended to benefit subsequent generations, to spare what is beautiful in the world from waste, from being trampled over by successive generations of laborers unable to spare a thought for the future.

Invoking the limitations of "shallow" ecology as contrasted with "deep" ecology, Una Chaudhuri finds that Astrov's (and Chekhov's) vision falls short. Articulated by the Norwegian philosopher Arne Næss, the concept of "shallow ecology" focuses on short-term fixes without questioning the consumption-oriented values and methods of the industrial economy that threaten the planet. These palliative measures might include the adoption of recycling programs or more stringent standards for automotive efficiency. "Deep ecology" refers to a radical reappraisal of humankind's place in and relationship to the environment, learning to see the environment in terms of its intrinsic value, not as merely a repository of resources of potential value for human use.[12] It emphasizes the pressing need for restructuring society according to a philosophy that ascribes to every living thing the same dignity, importance, and right to exist that we automatically ascribe to human beings. "For all his innate love of the forest," Chaudhuri argues, "Astrov cannot read his eco-maps ecologically, as a visual narrative of the ongoing destruction of nature by human beings; rather, he reads them as records of cultural deficiency."[13] For him, the only transcendent virtue is "beauty," and his ecology, Chaudhuri says, "supports the fiction — convenient to a consumerist economic system — that nature is an eco-machine, a virtual factory pouring out a stream of raw materials to be transformed into commodities."[14]

But beauty is not the enemy, and the pursuit of beauty need not be rejected as reifying a harmful division between nature

12 See Arne Næss, *Ecology, Community and Lifestyle: Outline of an Ecosophy*, trans. David Rothenberg (Cambridge: Cambridge University Press, 1989).
13 Una Chaudhuri, "'There Must Be a Lot of Fish in That Lake': Toward an Ecological Theater," *Theater* 25, no. 1 (1994): 24.
14 Ibid.

and the human. If we understand beauty to require a beholder, then indeed, it would appear that Astrov's dream is to have all the earth handsomely arrayed before spectators like himself, those refined enough to appreciate nature as a work of art. But beauty is not beauty because it is beheld. The sort of beauty Astrov is after is Kantian, "purposiveness […] without any representation of a purpose."[15] What Astrov adores about the forests is that they exist for their own sake, perfect unto themselves. They do not seek to be other than what they are. Unlike human beings, trees are not twisted up with anxiety about the meaning and purpose of their lives. Any purpose they have aside from being itself is projected onto them from without. Humans chopping them down and converting them into useful products is what destroys their beauty. The trees are unplagued by the desire to shape the landscape according to their vision and will and, accordingly, will never be beset by the shame of having destroyed something with a stronger claim to existence than them. For this, Astrov envies and admires them.

Human beings, on the other hand, demand more. They are forever making improvements, forever raising their standards, and they create for themselves lives that increasingly require more work to be sustained. Work occupies a central place in the imaginations of Chekhov's characters. It is scourge and salvation and everything in between, different things to different people, but always fundamental. Inquiring about the time Astrov invests in tending to the forests, Yelena asks, "it's important, I suppose, but doesn't it interfere with your real occupation? Being a doctor, I mean?" to which Astrov responds, "my real occupation? God only knows what that is."[16] Yelena, assuming that only the work one does for money can be a "real" occupation, is the opposite of inspired, industrious Astrov. She is constantly complaining of ennui. "If I don't find something to do, I'll die of boredom," she says.

---

15 Immanuel Kant, *Critique of Judgment*, trans. J. H. Bernard (London: Macmilland & Co., 1914), 90.
16 Chekhov, *Uncle Vanya*, 216.

SONYA: There's plenty to do. You just have to want to do it.
YELENA: Like *what*?
SONYA: Help out around the place, or go teach school, or go be a nurse. Isn't that enough? Before you and Papa came, Uncle Vanya and I used to take the flour to the market ourselves.
YELENA: I don't know how to do those things. Besides, I'm not interested. Going out to teach the poor, nursing them, all those high moral ideals — that only exists in books. What do you expect me to do, run out and teach, just like that?
SONYA: Frankly, I don't understand how you can *not* do something. You'd get used to it after a while.[17]

For Sonya there is never any question of whether to work or what to do. "We'll take whatever fate sends us," she tells Vanya in her closing speech, "[w]e'll spend the rest of our lives doing other people's work for them, we won't know a minute's rest, and then, when our time comes, we'll die. And when we're dead, we'll say that our lives were full of pain, that we wept and suffered, and God will have pity on us."[18]

Soviet ideologues have interpreted the play as an allegory of imminent class struggle, offering readings that identify Sonya as the *lumpenproletarian* who has partaken of the opiate of the masses and mistakes herself for some kind of martyr. For her, taking Christ as her pattern, life has meaning precisely because she has been persecuted and exploited. Yelena is the useless, decadent bourgeois, and Astrov, the revolutionary. He sees his medical practice as being relatively inconsequential, the treatment he provides for the suffering of individual men and women as being woefully short-term, compensatory, inadequate to the larger challenges of his age. He is prepared to dedicate himself to working towards a goal that may not be achievable in his lifetime. But the Soviet reading is overly anthropocentric.

17 Ibid., 232.
18 Ibid., 253.

Astrov's great love is not humanity, neither the bourgeoisie nor the workers. As Bataille's prehistoric man revered the animals he painted with greater care than he took with his self-portraits, Astrov reveres the trees, sees them as superior beings, perceives himself and all his kind as waste polluting their domain. This may be the deepest ecology of all.

"The Economy is the Crisis": Ibsen and Ostermeier's <u>Enemy of the People</u>

While Ibsen is not a deep ecologist, the plot of his *An Enemy of the People* (1882) also turns on questions of environmental waste, public health, and the priorities of civilization. After the play's titular "enemy" Doctor Stockmann discovers that his town's public baths have been dangerously contaminated, he attempts to make his findings public. Expecting to be hailed as a hero for blowing the whistle, Stockmann instead finds himself assailed from all sides by members of the community intent on preventing such a disclosure out of concern for the possible repercussions on the town's tourism economy. His brother and principle antagonist Mayor Stockmann opens the play trumpeting that said baths "will become the very life-principle of our town."[19] The brothers were both instrumental in the creation of the baths. The doctor is more of an idea guy, while the mayor was the one responsible for working out the practical details. Theirs is a fraternal quarrel which complicates the relationship between capitalism and self-interest. The mayor is a proponent of what will be referred to in another place and time as "trickle-down" economics. "The taxes for public welfare have been cut by a comfortable margin for the propertied classes," he explains, "and will be still more if we can only have a really good summer this year — hordes of visitors — masses of invalids who can give the baths a reputation."[20] The mayor appears to represent the

---

19 Henrik Ibsen, *An Enemy of the People,* in *Four Major Plays,* trans. Rolf Fjelde (New York: Penguin Books, 1970), 2:89.
20 Ibid., 90.

voice of common sense. The ailments and injuries of others are inarguably good for business. For the propertied classes.

During Doctor Stockmann's first tête-à-tête with his brother we learn that the two men are of different temperaments. The Mayor makes no attempt to conceal his disapproval of his brother's extravagant lifestyle. Offered roast beef and a hot toddy on an evening visit, he demurs in favor of bread, butter, and tea as "it's healthier in the long run — and a bit more economical too."[21] He is faintly repulsed by his brother's newfound joie de vivre. "I've been feeling so buoyant and happy," Doctor Stockmann exclaims controversially, "I can't tell you how lucky I feel to be part of this life that's budding and bursting out everywhere. What an amazing age we live in! It's as if a whole new world were rising around us!"[22] Having suffered through the pecuniary anxieties of the protracted adolescence that is graduate school, followed by a stint working a less lucrative job in a provincial town, Doctor Stockmann at last finds himself in a position to live large. While the doctor's drinking buddies fancifully aspire to being "Vikings" and "pagans," Mayor Stockmann efficiently conveys that he finds his brother's fondness for entertaining guests over meat and liquor to be both wasteful and immoral.[23] This petty contest primes us for the real conflict; Doctor Stockmann is planning to publish an article about the baths, making public the contamination he has discovered. His motives are not entirely pure — the doctor's article will be an indictment of his brother's implementation of the plans for the baths but will leave his own contribution, the general, sweeping vision, unsullied.

Doctor Stockmann is confident in his ability to persuade the town to rally behind him in part because he has faith in the "independent press." The motives of the press, however, are not entirely pure either. An editor tries to coerce Doctor Stockmann's daughter Petra into a romantic relationship on pain of his turning public opinion against her father. The lower-level

21 Ibid., 88.
22 Ibid., 93.
23 Ibid., 100.

editors who are so very enthusiastic about publishing the doctor's exposé are more interested in driving up readership with sensational material than with the actual public health crisis at hand. After languishing for some time at a sleepy local news bureau, the prospect of a "big scoop," whatever the consequences, is their primary motivator. Doctor Stockmann is also compromised by a conflict of interest between his sense of altruism and his ego. As the newspapermen are reviewing the proofs of his article, Stockmann cannot help but interject about the "parade" the townsfolk might be tempted to throw for him and how he hopes to be able to enlist all available help in quashing such a spectacle. His integrity is called into question when he reveals himself to still be, at heart, the underachieving little brother, hungry for recognition.

By Act Four, Doctor Stockmann has outgrown his ambitions as an environmental crusader; he has evolved into a radical philosopher, a self-styled, Nietzschean *Übermensch*. Effecting specific changes in his local community no longer appeals to him; he has bigger fish to fry, namely the transvaluation of all values. But at the town hall meeting he convenes, we hear speculative murmurs in the pre-show audience about how there might be a concealed "strain of insanity" in the family or about how "the man drinks."[24] Afterwards, Stockmann is paid a startling visit by his father-in-law Morten Kiil, a wealthy man whose not very eco-friendly tannery sits just upstream from the polluted baths, itself apparently responsible for much of the contamination. Kiil has just purchased newly cheap shares in the baths, sinking all of Mrs. Stockmann and the children's inheritance money into the very business venture Stockmann has spent the play trying to destroy. If he wants to guarantee the financial security of his family, Stockmann will have to renege on his crusade. The abstract good of clean water for all must be balanced against the concrete evil of poverty for one's own family.

The talent of the visionary is the ability to perceive the abstract as concrete, but Ibsen places equal emphasis on the bur-

24 Ibid., 173.

den that must be borne by the realists working to preserve the existing order, which the visionary too often forgets requires constant vigilance and effort just to maintain. At the end of Ibsen's play, after the entire Stockmann family has been put out of their jobs and ostracized for its patriarch's politically bungled attempt at whistle-blowing, Stockmann comes to the triumphant conclusion that "the strongest man in the world is the one who stands most alone."[25] His specific act of civic magnanimity is relinquished in favor of a great utopian project of progressive education, which he will pursue in the new world. Ibsen takes care to suggest, however, that this new visionary undertaking also stands a good chance of foundering on the shoals of reality. "Ah, come here, Katherine," Stockmann says to his wife, full of pride and hope, "look at that sunlight, how glorious, the way it streams in today. And how wonderful and fresh the spring air is." "Yes," she responds, "if only we could live on sunlight and spring air, Thomas."[26] The "new world" beckons, but in the new world, freedom is equated with "free" enterprise. Stockmann's wife and child will have to subsidize his refusal to capitulate to the will of the masses by living in poverty.

Ibsen wrote *Enemy of the People* immediately after his iconoclastic play *Ghosts* was met with a storm of reactionary criticism, and he almost certainly saw parts of himself in Doctor Stockmann. The saviors of the people will be perceived as enemies if they advocate for radical change, even if it is necessary change. But Ibsen is critical of Doctor Stockmann's deficiencies as a politician. Stockmann may welcome instability as a creative opportunity, but to achieve anything, he must understand that the majority will never respond well to the threat of chaos.

In his 2012 Schaubühne production of *Enemy of the People,* German director Thomas Ostermeier drives into this latent theme of the democratic political process. With large-scale ecological catastrophe presenting a far more pressing concern than it did in 1882, Ostermeier turns Ibsen's town hall scene into a

25 Ibid., 198.
26 Ibid., 196.

frame-breaking debate on the state of contemporary capitalism, with spectators encouraged to square off against the performers and each other. Ostermeier augments and updates Stockmann's town hall speech with references to the 2008 financial crisis: "The economy isn't in crisis. The economy is the crisis!" He also rails against the over-prescription of productivity-enhancing drugs such as Ritalin, European austerity programs, and the disintegration of the public sphere. As the production remains in the repertoire and tours, the catalogue of contemporary maladies evolves and expands.

Even as originally written by Ibsen this scene violates the economics of production by demanding a crowd of people onstage in a play that otherwise calls for only nine actors. Dramaturgically speaking, Ostermeier's town hall scene is a "wasteful" moment. If no one in the audience chooses to speak up, or if what they have to say is banal, irrelevant, or badly expressed, Ostermeier runs the risk of seeing his taut drama go slack. This was partially the case when the production toured to the Brooklyn Academy of Music in 2013. When large groups of strangers (the Harvey Theater seats 874) attempt to engage in open dialogue about their collective priorities, the result cannot but be somewhat chaotic. The voices that come to dominate are seldom the voices of the most informed. Complex and unfamiliar ideas take more courage and charisma to introduce successfully. It is easier to build consensus around negative observations than around positive proposals, easier to generate applause by calling for revolution than by laying out a plan for precisely how to balance the competing demands of economic development and environmental protection. Critique therefore carries the day, and it begins to become clear why policymaking is best conducted behind closed doors by a handful of specialists. Still, time-consuming as it is, articulating what a community does *not* value is a key step on the way to articulating what a community does value. The *Times* critic Charles Isherwood felt that the Brooklyn iteration of Ostermeier's town hall scene "derailed" the production.[27] But in creating a space for the messy, inefficient, and at times boring process of politics in a democratic society, Ostermeier eloquently demonstrates that wasted time is the price that should and must be paid to control the ecological waste threatening the townspeople of Ibsen's play, and, now, all of us. The shortsighted prioritization of efficiency and profits quickly turned will be far costlier in the long run. To survive, we must all become visionaries, capable of perceiving the abstract as concrete. Deep down, however, it seems we do not wish to survive.

Despoiled Shores

Heiner Müller's 1981 *Despoiled Shore Medea-material Landscape with Argonauts* is a landscape play in Gertrude Stein's sense. It is not that the landscape is a character; the play *is* a landscape. As such, it asks spectators for a different kind of engagement. Rather than presenting a human audience with representations of themselves to identify with, empathize with, project onto, the landscape play asks spectators to wander through, removing human subjectivity from the center of the event to the greatest extent possible. In our anthropocentric world, the landscape play offers spectators the increasingly unfamiliar opportunity to experience themselves as incidental.

In *Despoiled Shore,* unpardonable crimes against humanity are set beside crimes against nature. The modern world is a wasteland strewn with "torn menstrual napkins," "dead fish," "[c]ookie boxes," and "[f]eces."[28] It is populated by "children lay[ing] out landscapes with trash," "dead negroes," and "[z]ombies perforated by advertising spots."[29] Müller, who regularly works with scraps of the classics, chooses Euripides' *Me-*

---

27 Charles Isherwood, "An Ibsen Who Rages over Ritalin and Economic Austerity Plans," *New York Times,* November 7, 2013, https://www.nytimes.com/2013/11/08/theater/reviews/a-contemporary-enemy-of-the-people-at-the-harvey-theater.html.
28 Heiner Müller, *Hamletmachine and Other Texts for the Stage,* ed. and trans. Carl Weber (Baltimore: The Johns Hopkins University Press, 1984), 127.
29 Ibid., 134–35.

dea as an intertext here, giving us as our primary recognizable human being a mythological mother known for murdering her own children for spite. She is our image, the one we pretend we cannot see as we continue murdering the futures of subsequent generations, bringing the earth ever-closer to uninhabitability. Müller's stage directions note that the third part of the play, "Landscape with Argonauts," "presumes the catastrophes which mankind is working toward. The theatre's contribution to their prevention can only be their representation. The landscape might be a dead star where a task force from another age or another space hears a voice and discovers a corpse."[30] Earth's star has gone out. The undead survivors of the twentieth century who linger on are phantoms, beams of light that were extinguished long before they entered our field of vision. It is too late to put things right: "The youth of today ghosts of / The dead of the war that is to happen tomorrow / YET WHAT REMAINS IS CREATED BY BOMBS."[31] Humankind has fully relinquished control of its destiny to the technologies of destruction it has wrought. When Müller speaks of planned obsolescence, he refers to television sets and to bodies slated for the expiration in the predicted nuclear holocaust. Müller melds Medea with the despoiled landscape in this play; she speaks univocally with the earth. "A woman is the familiar ray of hope / BETWEEN THE THIGHS / DEATH STILL HAS HOPE" is her dark manifesto.[32] Hope for death? For an escape from death? This mother/earth refuses, as Bonnie Marranca puts it, to be "eternal," a utopia. She will no longer be an inexhaustible trove of resources for man, for children, for the imaginary of an exhausted civilization.

Pathological Superiority: Grasses of a Thousand Colors

Wallace Shawn has observed that, *pace* Darwin, humans "still haven't fully incorporated into our souls the idea that we're a

---

30 Ibid., 126.
31 Ibid., 134.
32 Ibid.

part of nature."³³ As a species, we have developed certain extraordinary abilities, and throughout history we have been more or less exultant about those special abilities and all that they have allowed us to accomplish. "Then in the twentieth century," Shawn says,

> it became clear that our special abilities made us capable of something unknown among the other species of the world — we seemed to have the ability to exterminate ourselves. Now in the twenty-first century, we see that our special abilities enable us to extinguish all living things and life itself. So the period of crowing about the marvelousness of our species has sort of come to an end.³⁴

This stubborn and pernicious conceptual divide between nature and the human is perpetuated by capitalism. Jason Moore argues that the Anthropocene is still not specific enough a term to describe the epoch of self-destruction in which we are currently living, proposing "Capitalocene" as a preferable alternative that takes into account capitalism's accumulation strategy: "Cheap Nature. For capitalism, Nature is 'cheap' in a double sense: to make Nature's elements 'cheap' in price; and also *to cheapen,* to degrade or to render inferior in an ethico-political sense."³⁵ Donna Haraway goes further still, suggesting "Chthulucene" as a better name, one that deprivileges the tragic human story and acknowledges that there was life before us and will be life after us. Our demise is not *the* end, only perhaps *an* end. The Chthulucene is made up of "ongoing multispecies stories and practices of becoming-with in times that remain at stake, in precarious times, in which the world is not finished and the sky has not fall-

---

33 Wallace Shawn, "The Art of Theater No. 17," interview by Hilton Als, *The Paris Review* 201 (Summer 2012), https://www.theparisreview.org/interviews/6154/wallace-shawn-the-art-of-theater-no-17-wallace-shawn.
34 Ibid.
35 Jason W. Moore, *Anthropocene or Capitalocene? Nature, History, and the Crisis of Capitalism* (Oakland: PM Press, 2016), 2–3.

en—yet."³⁶ Even if our time is up, we can and should still work to improve the lot of those other beings. To ignore our kinship with them is to insist on bringing what we call the natural world down with us. In his *Grasses of a Thousand Colors* Shawn imagines a world finally expiring after suffering through the long illness of this imposed nature/society binary.

Grasses is narrated mainly by Ben, played by Shawn in the 2013 Public Theater production. Early on, Ben informs us that his own dick is his best friend, perhaps his only real friend. The most significant relationship Ben has with a separate life form is his intense, sexual relationship with a cat named Blanche. The play juxtaposes narrated scenes of wild, interspecies, orgiastic rites with piecemeal hints at the novel method the human race has found for exterminating itself. In addition to being a man of rather peculiar sexual predilections, Ben is a megalomaniacal scientist who doesn't see himself that way. His optimistic generation of fixers and improvers "solved" the problem of food scarcity by engineering a set of biological and ecological modifications that made it possible for animals (and, we are left to assume, humans) to live off the flesh of their own kind and to multiply at accelerated rates. Ben's scientific contributions to the new cannibalistic world order have made him wealthy — and backfired spectacularly. With the food chain disrupted, animals are dropping dead in droves and humans are heading in that direction, incapacitated by increasingly frequent bouts of vomiting. Such eventualities were made to seem not at all improbable by rhyming real-world events that began appearing in the news after *Grasses* premiered — half of the endangered Saiga antelope population mysteriously dying in the space of two weeks in Kazakhstan in 2015, for example. As Elizabeth Kolbert demonstrates in *The Sixth Extinction*, by the end of the twenty-first century, human activity will have resulted in the elimination of twenty to fifty percent of all living species on earth. *Grasses* presents an impressionistic picture of the Anthropocene (or

---

36 Donna Haraway, *Staying with the Trouble: Making Kin in the Chthulucene* (Durham: Duke University Press, 2016), 55.

Capitalocene or Chthulucene) period unfurling; the fact that "humans change the world" is our distinction if not our honor.[37]

Though in *Grasses*, Ben is presented as the principle architect of this cataclysm, he disavows all responsibility, and the play instead focuses on his extensive erotic adventures and misadventures. With world hunger vanquished, it seems overpopulation no longer presents the threat it once did, and the libidinously turbocharged planet seems determined to go down in a blaze of orgasmic glory. The basic drives — for food and sex — have been thrown out of whack. Perhaps the body revolts at the suggestion that it could experience both hunger and sexual desire for the same kind of creature. In *Grasses* it is as though sex (in all kinds of surreal and occasionally unvisualizable configurations) comes rushing in to fill the void left by nourishment of the caloric variety. The farther the human race gets from "nature" or the "natural order," the closer humans are, perversely, drawn back to it. The play ends in a swamp of abjection, and it ultimately becomes impossible to distinguish between the human and the animal. In the Public Theater production, projections of Julie Haggerty, the actress playing Ben's wife Cerise, show her slowly morphing into a cat (*the* cat?) as she sends messages from a refuge in the countryside where she has fled to escape the horrors of the pandemic. All that remains is the residue of humanity, the traces of the destruction the human species has left in its wake. Just before the end of a play, Cerise/Blanche shows Ben a photo album, the book of his life, a record of his legacy. The photographs show only "black landscapes, covered with — naked? — well, they were dead animals, I guess, cats and other animals, but the bodies were misshapen, bloated, the skin was broken." Shortly thereafter, Ben adds his own corpse to the pile. In contrast to the violent, painful deaths of the animals, Ben's demise is depicted as peaceful, welcome, even beautiful; Cerise/Blanche leads him out to an open field and soothingly explains as he lays himself down that "while vomiting was awful,

---

37 Elizabeth Kolbert, *The Sixth Extinction: An Unnatural History* (New York: Henry Holt and Company, 2014), 266.

and suffering was awful, death in itself was a trivial process, […] She herself had been through it a number of times, and it was literally nothing." Blanche/Cerise seems to exist on some kind of magical morphological continuum that transcends the confines of time and space. She is woman, animal, dead, alive, animate, inanimate, past, present, and future. Ben is bounded by his body, wholly identified with his penis and its hopes and dreams. "Most things," Blanche/Cerise continues, "aren't alive in the first place, and they never were, […] it's not particularly tragic to be a chair or a rock, and obviously the spark of life which occasionally flares up will inevitably go out, and it's not a problem, and it doesn't call for a hysterical response."[38] Human, Shawn posits in *Grasses, is* a kind of generalized hysterical condition, rather than a superior, or even distinct, kind of organism.

What has long been considered superior about the human species ends by tipping over into its opposite. As Benjamin's angel of history confronts us with the products of human progress, the waste of progress, *Grasses* stages the terminus of human evolution, suggesting the possibility that perhaps humanity has been merely a great cancerous growth that spread, devouring everything its path. Aware on some level that we are sick, that we are a sickness, we divide and divide, seeking to keep at least one group between ourselves and the animals with whom we must deny kinship. Only the need for food and the need for sex persist as constant reminders that we are made of the same stuff. We need the lie but feel ashamed for needing it, so are always on the lookout for those whose repudiation of animality, of nature, can be identified as insufficient, flawed, and therefore subhuman.

Posthuman Otherness

Woman has historically been seen as closer to animality and therefore less human than Man. For Aristotle, women were more impulsive, inferior to men in strength and virtue, and less

---

38 Ibid., 88.

prone to shame. Throughout the medieval period, women were believed to have "weak intellects."[39] For Freud, the trouble was that women took a "very circuitous path" to psychosexual developmental maturity and were consequently left only imperfectly capable of sublimation. The gendering of Shawn's radical gesture towards the posthuman in the figure of Blanche/Cerise recalls Müller's treatment of Medea or *The Task*'s lady Liberty. Like Müller's men, Shawn's Ben epitomizes a particular totalizing, ossified, outmoded genre of male subjectivity, one that is shown in *Grasses* to be a contributing cause of the end of life on earth. In the final moments of *Grasses*, as in *Despoiled Shore,* Woman's otherness is sought out as a last resort — only after the white, bourgeois, heterosexual male narratives appear to have exhausted themselves. This is a dramaturgical move at least as old as *Faust,* drawn ever-onward and -upward by his "eternal" feminine. Having long interpreted their experiences through those of men, the ones that get written down and called "neutral" or "universal," women are always already (at least) bilingual. An authentic encounter with alterity, Emmanuel Levinas writes, is the most revealing experience of our own humanity that it is possible to have; we experience ourselves as profoundly *responsible* for the other, "infinitely responsible." It is a responsibility, he writes, "to which I am wanting and faulty. It is as though I were responsible for his mortality, and guilty for surviving."[40] In psychoanalytic terms, survivor's guilt emerges from the self perceiving itself as excessive, unjustified, and somehow existentially unjust — waste, a remainder rendered meaningless without those to and for whom he was responsible. When Woman is simply called in to clean up after the men have made a mess of things, we see "responsibility" flowing, again, in just one direction, and from the Levinasian perspective it is precisely the wrong direction. Finally, they each in their own way arrive at a

---

39 Teresa of Ávila, *Book of My Life,* trans. Mirabai Starr (Boston: New Seeds Books, 2007), 89.

40 Emmanuel Levinas, *Otherwise Than Being,* trans. A. Lingis (Dordrecht: Njihoff, 1974), 91.

reconciliation of Levinas's dictum that "ethics precedes ontology" and the possibilities of posthumanism. A posthumanist worldview admits that the human is not the center of existence. Humans have never been entirely distinct from animals, and they are coming to more closely resemble machines with each passing day. Individual human beings are forged in the differentiating crucibles of culture and history. The posthumanist takes the view that there is nothing universal about the human essence and that, therefore, humanism is both theoretically and practically incoherent. Fukuyama may have been right. But if we are post-history, it is not because we are post-ideology but because we are post-human.

Rachel Rosenthal's Ecofeminism

A growing body of research suggests that climate change skepticism is bound up with antifeminism. Climate change deniers perceive that the real threat is to a certain kind of modern industrial masculinity and not to the environment.[41] Egalitarian concern for the latter is seen as feminine, while the observation of a hierarchical separation between humans and nature is seen as more masculine. The ecofeminist performance artist Rachel Rosenthal thematizes this strand of misogyny, harnessing her myriad experiences of otherness to conjure transformative empathy for the earth. If women have been thought to derive their superior compassion — their intuition of the interconnectedness of all things — from their experience of realized or potential maternity, Rosenthal deconstructs this essentialism. She does not celebrate the pleasing or pleasurable aspects of womanhood. Instead, she elevates the difficult, and even mortifying dimensions of occupying her queer, female-gendered body. It is her suffering that connects her with the suffering of the world, and she claims the earth as her kin while distancing herself from

---

41 Jonas Anshelm and Martin Hultman, "A Green Fatwā? Climate Change As a Threat to the Masculinity of Industrial Modernity," NORMA: *International Journal for Masculinity Studies* 9, no. 2 (2014): 85.

the conventional signifiers of femininity. In Rosenthal's 1990 solo piece *Pangaean Dreams: A Shamanic Journey,* she overlays a meditation on the sundering of the original single continent of the earth, Gaia, with autobiographical rage and revelations having to do with the more humiliating and revolting aspects of being female. Rosenthal engages in a dialogue with the chronic pain that plagues her, rendering that pain as a character she calls the Autonomous Being. She places her broken body in conversation with the broken world and finds affinity in their shared finitude.

Performing solo into her seventies, Rosenthal asked spectators to confront the specter of the aging female body in a way seldom required of them. Our culture has turned the postmenopausal female body into a kind of *memento mori.* William Viney has argued that when we consign an object to the garbage can, we are situating ourselves within a narrative of "use-time." As something becomes waste, "[m]atter, and thus time, becomes organized in relation to our activities of human use and non-use, by a temporal separation structured by what is considered unproductive and uninhabited."[42] Rosenthal recognizes that this temporal separation is applied to the bodies of women and their perceived expiration dates as well. In her piece *L.O.W. in Gaia,* Rosenthal identifies herself as the "Crone," hated by all because her body, unable to bring forth life, conjures death. Even while the evidence of female fertility in the form of menstrual blood is among the most feared and loathed of human waste products, the infertile female is herself consigned to the category of human waste. For the Crone reminds us, as Rosenthal puts it, not of heroic or "meaningful" death, but of the decidedly unglamorous deaths most of us die, preceded by disease and decrepitude, a slow slide into mortifying passivity and obsolescence. Rosenthal uses her dying body as a metaphor for the dying earth, a victim of masculine violence, attempted commodification, and exploitative technologies.

---

42 William Viney, *Waste: A Philosophical History of Things* (London: Bloomsbury, 2014), 21.

Stifters Dinge: Posthuman Theater

Samuel Beckett is quoted by one of his biographers as saying that "[t]he best possible play is one in which there are no actors, only the text. I'm trying to find a way to write one."[43] The German composer and director Heiner Goebbels may have come closest to achieving Beckett's dream with his 2007 performance installation *Stifters Dinge*, a play for a posthuman world. Inspired by the writings of the nineteenth-century Austrian writer Adalbert Stifter, the piece is performed by five mechanized pianos on a dynamic set that evokes the world without us. Goebbels is less interested in Beckett's formal perfection than in the implications for culture of the self-inflicted extinction of the human being.

Stifter's writings are distinguished by their tremulously vivid and detailed descriptions of the natural world. Long passages tracing the changing light reflecting off of a glacier, the veins of a leaf, or the texture of a stone assume more narrative prominence than any account of human action or awareness. The revulsion Stifter felt for industrial modernity manifested itself in his texts as a profound reverence for *things,* animate or inanimate. His landscape writing created a context for letting the diverse insentient beings of the world be, to let being itself be, as Heidegger would put it. As capitalism advances and accelerates, pulverizing and clearing that which cannot be commodified, Stifter's humble, elegiac observations rescue things from being captured and either exploited for profit or destroyed. Cradled in his receptive consciousness, things become eloquent, their very lack of subjectivity elevating them to a plane of existence surpassing perfection, the plane of the sublime.

Goebbels translates Stifter's prose for the stage into music and images that invite the spectator to reduce her customary pace to the speed of insects, growing moss, melting snow. The sounds

---

43 Walter Kerr, "The Love between Beckett and Actors Isn't Mutual," *New York Times*, November 13, 1988, https://www.nytimes.com/1988/11/13/theater/stage-view-the-love-between-beckett-and-actors-isn-t-mutual.html.

issuing from the disemboweled pianos include harsh sounds of machinery, snatches of Bach melodies, mysterious percussion, and recorded human voices speaking or singing across time and space in a variety of languages. A long, recorded passage of Stifter's prose is played, describing the sound of thousands of frozen tree branches rattling against one another like so many bells chiming. The first and last time we see human beings is when two unobtrusive technicians dressed in black enter at the top of the show to sprinkle what appears to be salt or sand into shallow troughs covering the floor of what we would call the "playing space" in a different kind of production. The technicians leave, and hoses fill the troughs with water. The mise-en-scène is then dominated by rippling smoke on water, projected images of landscape paintings, and the slow, eerie movement of entire set. The elaborately mutilated player pianos sit on platforms out of which barren trees also grow, and this whole apparatus gradually glides on a track towards the audience, until it is just feet from the first row. Its approach feels like the imminent end of the world. But then, unexpectedly, the trees and pianos recede, eventually resuming their original position upstage. As we witness this movement, we hear the recorded voice of Claude Lévi-Strauss say, "I don't believe there is any reason" to have faith in humankind. The trees and the music of the icicles cracking and falling from their branches will persist even after we have exterminated ourselves. The spectator, the excess, the human is incidental.

4

Debt and the Refugee

In *Wasted Lives: Modernity and Its Outcasts*, Zygmunt Bauman argues that, along with traditional industrial waste, refugees, migrants, the chronically unemployed, and other such groups of "undesirables" are "the waste of globalization."[1] The fate of this "human waste" is the price necessarily paid for what we call progress. It no longer makes sense to speak of discrete refugee crises; it seems likely that we have entered a period of perpetual refugee crisis. If the legacy of colonialism and Western military intervention in the developing world were not enough to create massive instability and displacement, the intensifying climate crisis has begun the process of rendering the earth uninhabitable. As we wait for the water wars to begin in earnest, populations facing extreme weather and increasingly unreliable access to vital natural resources will continue to uproot their families and set out for lands perceived to be more stable, more wealthy, and generally better equipped to withstand the approaching catastrophe.

The mass human "waste" produced by this malignant triad — imperialism, war, and ecological disaster — is regularly invoked by right-wing politicians as a hostile enemy force that

---

1 Zygmunt Bauman, *Wasted Lives: Modernity and Its Outcasts* (New York: Polity Press, 2003), 5.

has arisen independent of Western activities. In September of 2015 as the European Union was staring down an accelerating refugee situation, Polish MEP (Member of the European Parliament) Janusz Korwin-Mikke took to the European Parliament floor to rail against welfare policies perceived as facilitating the influx of migrants:

> If we were to abolish social benefits, there wouldn't be any people coming to Poland and the whole Europe [sic] just to live off of handouts. People willing to work are valuable, but they are being sent back to their countries and we take in those unwilling to work. This is a ridiculous policy that results in Europe being flooded with human garbage.[2]

"Let's state this clear," he continued for emphasis, "*human garbage* that does not want to work. The America [sic] built its power because it took in immigrants willing to work and did not give any handouts. We are ruining Europe."[3] Around the same time, British Prime Minister David Cameron warned of a "swarm of people coming across the Mediterranean." Donald Trump prefers to describe asylum-seekers and migrants in terms of floods and flows, though he has also used the term "shithole countries" to describe their homelands.[4] By metaphorically linking the refugee with plague, pestilence, and filth, such language de-individuates and strips its referents of human qualities, making it easier to incite xenophobic fear.

The contagion visited by the dirty outsider, at best a useless freeloader, at worst a violent menace, has become a danger invoked constantly by the Western liberal democracies Fukuyama

---

2 BreakingNews, "Deputy Describes as 'Human Garbage' Syrian Refugees in Europe," *Metatube*, September 13, 2015, https://www.metatube.com/en/videos/284161/Deputy-describes-as-human-garbage-Syrian-refugees-in-Europe/.
3 Ibid.
4 Julie Hirschfeld Davis et al., "Trump Alarms Lawmakers with Disparaging Words for Haiti and Africa," *New York Times*, January 11, 2018, https://www.nytimes.com/2018/01/11/us/politics/trump-shithole-countries.html.

extols. When refugees are not being linked to literal human waste, they are often discussed in terms of waste management or elimination. After the Obama administration announced in 2015 that the US would take in at least ten thousand Syrian refugees over the following year, the *New York Times* reported that at a hearing to address community concerns about the coming influx in one South Carolina town,

> a woman asked if the refugees could be sent home on "troop ships." A man asked if they could be sent on a plane to Saudi Arabia. When he was told that they could not, his frustration mounted. "Do we shoot them?" he asked, to laughter and applause. "Come on! I mean, this is crazy."[5]

White Americans alarmed by the changing demographics of their communities found their champion in a man hitherto a stranger to politics aside from his sole credit as high-profile propagator of the "birther" movement, designed to delegitimize the first black president by calling on Barack Obama to release his birth certificate. Ostensibly motivated by the desire to verify that Obama was in fact born in the United States, the goal of birtherism was to remind Americans that, no matter where they were born, how accomplished or how devoted to public service they are, black people are not "real" Americans. Donald Trump kicked off his bid for the Republican presidential nomination by conjuring the threat of the violent, amoral immigrant as he articulated his vision for "making America great again," opining that

> [w]hen Mexico sends its people, they're not sending the best — they're not sending you. They're sending people that have lots of problems and they're bringing those problems.

---

5 Richard Fausset, "Refugee Crisis in Syria Raises Fears in South Carolina," *New York Times*, September 25, 2015, https://www.nytimes.com/2015/09/26/us/refugee-crisis-in-syria-raises-fears-in-south-carolina.html.

> They're bringing drugs. They're bringing crime. They're rapists. And some, I assume, are good people.⁶

Trump later called for an outright ban on Muslims entering the United States. Ignoring the irreversible damage automation has done to unskilled workers in the US manufacturing sector, Trump instead redirected the anger of Rust Belt Americans staring down increasingly precarious economic futures toward the Chinese, whom he often characterized as "stealing our jobs" and, contrary to longstanding conservative orthodoxy, Trump campaigned on a platform of trade isolationism.

The nationalist and nativist resurgence, with the attendant calls for razor wire fences and walls, followed a predictable pattern, coming on the heels of a financial crisis that had bedeviled Europe and the US since 2008. The European Union had appeared to be teetering on the precipice of dissolution during the Greek debt crisis, and then in the June 2016 "Brexit" referendum Britons voted to abandon ship. And then Trump won.

Once he took office, Trump's administration instituted a "zero tolerance" policy for illegal immigration, meaning that anyone crossing the border unlawfully would be prosecuted to the full extent of a law only selectively enforced under previous administrations. At the same time, many designated ports of entry were closed to asylum seekers attempting to enter the US legally. As a result, thousands of children were separated from their parents at the border separating the US and Mexico. Parents were dispatched to be prosecuted and deported while their minor children were forcibly taken from them by US Customs and Border Protection and held in chain-link cages. Newly unaccompanied infants and toddlers were sent to one of three "tender age shelters" in southern Texas. The response from the international community was swift and damning. United Na-

---

6 Alexander Burns, "Choice Words from Donald Trump, Presidential Candidate," *New York Times,* June 16, 2015, https://www.nytimes.com/politics/first-draft/2015/06/16/choice-words-from-donald-trump-presidential-candidate/.

tions High Commissioner for Human Rights Zeid Ra'ad Al Hussein called on the US to end the practice, explaining that "the American Association of Pediatrics has called this cruel practice 'government-sanctioned child abuse' which may cause 'irreparable harm,' with 'lifelong consequences.'" The thought that any State would seek to deter parents by inflicting such abuse on children is unconscionable."[7]

In response, the US withdrew from the Human Rights Council. While Trump officially ended the policy of family separation by executive order in June 2018, and a federal judge ordered Immigration and Customs Enforcement to reunite the children with their parents by the end of July 2018, the deadline came and went with many children remaining in limbo. Some affected families spoke no English or Spanish, only indigenous languages, making translation more difficult, and of course many of the "tender age" detainees had no access to language of any kind. Having already deported hundreds of parents back to countries such as Honduras and Guatemala, the Trump administration had no immediately apparent way of locating them or reconnecting them with their children. By the summer of 2019 Border Patrol was still detaining thousands of children at a time in overcrowded facilities without adequate food or access to showers or toothbrushes. Holocaust survivor Yoka Verdoner wrote that the border separations were "as evil and criminal as what happened to me and my siblings as children in Nazi Europe."[8]

---

[7] Zeid Ra'ad Al Hussein, "Opening Statement and Global Update of Human Rights Concerns by UN High Commissioner for Human Rights Zeid Ra'ad Al Hussein at 38th Session of the Human Rights Council," *United Nations Human Rights Council*, June 18. 2018, https://www.ohchr.org/EN/HRBodies/HRC/Pages/NewsDetail.aspx?NewsID=23206&LangID=E.

[8] Yoka Verdoner, "Nazis Separated Me from My Parents as a Child. The Trauma Lasts a Lifetime," *The Guardian*, June 18, 2018, https://www.theguardian.com/commentisfree/2018/jun/18/separation-children-parents-families-us-border-trump.

WASTE

Fassbinder and West German Schuld

Without endorsing the equivalence Verdoner suggests in her comparison, it is clear that the two atrocities shared a symbolic language. The Holocaust was a tragedy of waste made possible by the conversion of great swaths of humanity — Jews, communists, so-called "gypsies," homosexuals, the disabled — into literal and metaphorical waste, garbage to be disposed of in order to cleanse and strengthen the surviving Aryan race. For Nazi functionaries to send their victims to the gas chamber, the Jew's status as a human had first to be comprehensively undermined. She was no longer an individual but a unit of rubbish. Acquiring the power to enact this transfiguration in one's mind was a part of an S.S. officer's on-the-job training. In *Life Unworthy of Life: Racial Phobia and Mass Murder in Hitler's Germany,* James M. Glass relates how

> Franz Stangl, commandant of Treblinka [in German-occupied Poland], described the moment he began to think of the Jews under his supervision not as humans, but as "cargo": "I think it started the day I first saw the *Totenlager* [burial pits] in Treblinka. I remember Wirth [who oversaw exterminations in Belsen, Sobibor, and Treblinka] standing there, next to the pits full of blue-black corpses. It had nothing to do with humanity — it couldn't have; it was a mass — a mass of rotting flesh. Wirth said, "What shall we do with this garbage?... I rarely saw them as individuals. It was always a huge mass."[9]

West German playwright and filmmaker Rainer Werner Fassbinder was born in 1945, just weeks after the end of the Second World War, making him a part of the first generation of Germans to fully grapple with their nation's guilt. Fassbinder made no attempt to represent the Holocaust directly, an aesthetic en-

---

9 James M. Glass, *Life Unworthy of Life: Racial Phobia and Mass Murder in Hitler's Germany* (New York: Basic Books, 1997), 9.

deavor many judge to be either impossible, obscene, or both. Instead, Fassbinder assiduously ferreted out the underlying anxieties that made the rise of fascism possible, paying particular attention to those that survived the Second World War and continued to plague West German society. The *Endlösung* or "Final Solution" was not, after all, conceived as a meaningless inferno of waste but as an efficient way to make Germany great again by purging it of "unproductive" members of society. The surviving German valorization of efficiency, Fassbinder worried, might prove more insidiously deadly than overt anti-Semitism.

In his 1975 play *Garbage, the City, and Death,* Fassbinder uses grotesquely amplified, stereotypical characters and attitudes to foreground the racially directed, economic fears that served as a pretext for the consolidation of Nazi influence and eventually for the Holocaust. The Jewish people have variously been blamed for the worst excesses of capitalism, communism, and anything else for which insecure societies have required a scapegoat throughout human history. Jews have been suspected both of orchestrating the Bolshevik Revolution as part of a conspiracy for world domination and, more commonly, of siphoning capital away from "productive" members of society with their supposedly usurious lending practices and generally mercenary way of life. Even Marx, himself ancestrally Jewish, was convinced that "[m]oney is the jealous god of Israel, beside which no other god may exist. Money abases all the gods of mankind and changes them into commodities. […] Money is the alienated essence of man's work and existence; this essence dominates him and he worships it. The god of the Jews has been secularized and has become the god of this world."[10] If is to some degree true that Jews have historically gravitated to professions such as banking and law, this is in large part due to millennia of anti-Semitic restrictions placed on the rights of Jews to own property, a precondition for the pursuit of occupations traditionally seen as more "wholesome" or productive, such as agriculture. Promul-

---

10 Karl Marx, "On the Jewish Question," in *The Marx–Engels Reader,* ed. Robert C. Tucker (New York: Norton, 1978), 50.

gating the stereotype of the urban, nomadic, parasitic Jew who lacks the properly moral and patriotic connection to land and country was one of the ways in which the Nazis were able to sow the suspicion and fear they needed to win their propaganda war against the Jewish people.

In *Garbage, the City, and Death* Fassbinder hypostatizes the persistent German paranoia about Jewish economic influence *after* the Second World War. Seyla Benhabib has observed that making the character of the Nazi in the play a transvestite, "someone who becomes something at night that he is not during the day," reflects the way Fassbinder saw West German society, where he found "fascism lurking beneath the complacent exterior of technocratic capitalism."[11] One character rails against the threat posed by another figure identified only as the Rich Jew:

> He's sucking us dry, the Jew. Drinking our blood and blaming everything on us because he's a Jew and we're guilty. I rack my brains and I brood. I tear at my nerves. I'm going under. I wake up nights, my throat like it's in a noose, death stalking me in person. My reason tells me they're just images, myths fromthe pre-history of our fathers. I feel a sharp pain on my left side. My heart, I ask myself? Or the gallbladder? And it's the Jew's fault. Just being there he makes us guilty. If he stayed where he came from or if they gassed him I'd be able to sleep better. They forgot to gas him. […] He's always one step ahead and all he leaves us is charity. Garbage, worthless objects.[12]

Forty years after it was written and nearly eighty years after the Holocaust, *Garbage* is still considered too incendiary for any

---

11 Seyla Benhabib, Andrei Makovitz, and Moishe Postone, "Rainer Werner Fassbinder's *Garbage, the City and Death*: Renewed Antagonisms in the Complex Relationship between Jews and Germans in the Federal Republic of Germany," *New German Critique* 38 (1986): 17.

12 Rainer Werner Fassbinder, *Garbage, The City and Death*, in *Plays*, ed. Denis Calandra (Baltimore: The Johns Hopkins University Press, 1985), 180.

theater to risk a production in Germany. In part because of the public outcry elicited by the play's premiere, much of the criticism of *Garbage* has focused on the question of whether the play is itself anti-Semitic. But as the equally provocative German theater-and-filmmaker Christoph Schlingensief put it, sometimes a sick society needs strong medicine:

> As the son of a pharmacist, what I often say is that my father cured people with minute amounts of poison. He gave them poison so that their bodies could right themselves. And I think that's how we should understand images of Germany. When I'm making a film I would like to know what disease I'm dealing with.[13]

The offensive elements of *Garbage* function as minute amounts of inoculating poison, intended to treat the disease of lingering German anti-Semitism. The economic anxiety that Fassbinder hits on in the play is intentionally elided with another, much more profound anxiety. After the Holocaust, will the German not be "in debt" to the Jew forever? The crime is of such proportions that German guilt can never be expiated. The symbolic slippage between monetary and moral debt is particularly potent in German as the word *Schuld* means both "debt" and "guilt."

In interrogating the prejudices and predilections that turned Germany against its Jewish population, Fassbinder finds that many of the same violent, exclusionary impulses that led to the Holocaust persist in the form of "everyday fascism." Spiritually, Germany is internally riven, divided against itself, sadomasochistic. The German hates the Jew not because the Jew is Other, but because the German is the Jew. The Jew is part of her. So the Jew must be punished, tortured, exterminated. Other vulnerable groups suffer as a result of the same (il)logic. The man hates the woman, the heterosexual the homosexual, the native

---

13 Frieder Schlaich, *Christoph Schlingensief and His Films* (Berlin: Filmgaleri 451, 2005).

the immigrant. *Garbage* features a cast of characters made up of criminals, prostitutes and other sexual "deviants," and uncouth foreigners. A character identified only as the "Dwarf" completes the menagerie. He is drawn to vulnerable outsiders, "B people" or "subway people," people who live much of their lives "underground" either to protect themselves from scorn and violence or because they have been left out or pushed out by the dominant culture. What these marginalized groups have in common is the ability to attract the revulsion of mainstream society, which perceives them as unproductive leeches on its otherwise healthy, productive body. Defending himself against charges of anti-Semitism during the *Garbage* controversy, Fassbinder advised his critics to consider the consistent support for oppressed minorities demonstrated throughout his oeuvre.

Indeed, one of his earliest plays, *Katzelmacher* (which translates as "Cock Artist"), is a pure parable of xenophobia's evils. Written in the vein of Marieluise Fleißer and Ödön von Horváth, playwrights who engaged critically with the *Volksstücke* ("Folk Play") tradition in the 1920s and '30s, *Katzelmacher* explores the ways in which the poisonous atmosphere of insular, provincial life abrades language and thought. In *Katzelmacher*, a small, homogenous German town is shaken when a Greek named Jorgos arrives as a guest worker. Animosity blossoms instantly. Fassbinder weaves together sexual and economic rivalries to illustrate the multiple levels on which fear of the other tends to operate. Jorgos's roommate Bruno, a native, plants the first seed of panic and intrigue in the community:

BRUNO: He's "foreign labor."
ERICH: What that?
BRUNO: Like I said, "foreign labor."[14]

In Germany, the term used here, *Fremdarbeiter,* has strong negative connotations and was in widespread use during the Nazi

14 Rainer Werner Fassbinder, *Katzelmacher,* in *Plays,* ed. Denis Calandra (Baltimore: The Johns Hopkins University Press, 1985), 80.

period. After the war, it was replaced by the term *Gastarbeiter* or "guest worker," which is now used in all official contexts. Fassbinder's characters struggle with the terminology and perceived threat of competition:

> ERICH: What's that supposed to mean? Don't we have enough workers?
> BRUNO: A Greek from Greece.
> ERICH: No way. That ain't fair no how.
> BRUNO: Right.
> ERICH: We work too. Plenty.
> PAUL: He cut in on you yet, with Elisabeth?
> GUNDA: Where's he sleep?
> BRUNO: My room.
> ERICH: Your room. How come?
> BRUNO: There was a bunk, that's how come.
> PAUL: Did he talk to you, yet?
> BRUNO: He can't talk. But when he goes to bed he strips. All the way.
> PAUL: No!
> BRUNO: Right.
> GUNDA: With you there?
> BRUNO: He doesn't know any better.
> ERICH: What's he look like?
> BRUNO: Better than us.
> ERICH: How better?
> BRUNO: Better built.
> ERICH: Where?
> BRUNO: In the cock.[15]

This disclosure sends Gunda, the sole woman in their clique present, running straight to Jorgos. But Gunda later characterizes their subsequent sexual encounter as a brutal rape, presumably in an attempt to shield herself from the censure of the envious and intimidated local men.

15 Ibid.

In *Katzelmacher*, Jorgos ultimately falls victim to such rage. The local men disparage him for many things — he can't speak German, doesn't bathe, is a communist, and is taking their jobs. An exchange regarding this last fear anticipates economic imbalances that will later be exacerbated by accelerating globalization, but the winners and losers don't stack up the way the natives assume they do:

> BRUNO: [The boss] says it's better for business.
> ERICH: If he stays.
> BRUNO: Right, because it's true.
> GUNDA: How come?
> BRUNO: Because we produce more now, and she only pays him six hundred fifty marks. He sleeps in my room and she deducts a hundred fifty marks for that.
> GUNDA: A hundred fifty. That's allowed?
> BRUNO: Right. And for food another hundred eighty. That comes to three hundred thirty marks. She pays him three hundred twenty marks.
> ERICH: Not bad.
> BRUNO: That's what the man from the foreign labor department in Munich told her. You have to do it that way because then it's more productive because they're here and the money stays in the country.
> ERICH: So that's how it is.
> BRUNO: Right. It's a trick. For Germany's sake.[16]

Today it is no longer nations, which at least ostensibly answer to their body politic, but rather multinational corporations, which answer only to their shareholders, that get to keep the big money.

The townspeople in *Katzelmacher* do not or cannot articulate what it is that fuels their blind and murderous resentment of the stranger in their midst, but after Jorgos has slept with every woman in the play, the men savagely beat him (after first en-

---

16 Ibid., 92.

tertaining the possibility of castrating him) in an act of dumb, brutish, male jealousy. Jorgos is no choir boy—he has a family back in Greece and is betraying his wife with every woman in town—but when Fassbinder made the play into a film, he played the role of Jorgos himself, indicating a special affinity for the character.

The gender dynamics Fassbinder perceives as motivating xenophobia have been on display during the recent European refugee crisis, when the issue of women's safety was once again taken up as a justification for the nationalistic backlash against Arab and North-African asylum seekers in Germany. In an incident on 2015–2016 New Year's Eve at Cologne's central train station, as many as a thousand women were, reportedly, sexually assaulted by groups of men who appeared to belong mostly to the refugees' demographics. Troubling as the allegations were, the response was worse: right-wing traditionalists tend to exhibit concern for the rights of women only when they can be used as a cudgel to advance other aspects of a conservative agenda. Wherever xenophobia flourishes, wounded masculinity is transformed into skepticism about the possibilities of cultural integration. Calls for racial purity soon follow.

Sarah Kane's Blasted and the Bedrock of Sexual Difference

Sarah Kane's *Blasted* depicts the explosive entrance of a refugee figure as the return of what the West has repressed, but the play is also a poetic indictment of violence in all its forms. *Blasted* unequivocally embraces Levinas's concept of "infinite responsibility," making no attempt to conceal the cost. Set in an expensive hotel room in the middle of a war zone, the first half of the play is dominated by Ian, a tabloid journalist who dredges up gory "human interest" stories with the potential to sell papers. We overhear him dictating one about an attractive young British woman being gruesomely murdered by foreigners while abroad. Sensational journalism, however, is only a cover for his real occupation, which involves driving getaway cars and covertly disposing of bodies for the government.

The respect Ian feels is his due is entirely contingent on contesting the humanity of others. Kane quickly establishes him as racist ("Hate this city. Stinks. Wogs and Pakis taking over"), contemptuous of the disabled ("Retard isn't he? [...] Aye. Spaz. [...] Glad my son's not a Joey"), and homophobic ("Hitler was wrong about the Jews who have they hurt the queers he should have gone for scum them").[17] In the first few minutes of the play, he commands Cate, his young, simple-minded lover to perform oral sex on him. When she refuses, he assumes that it is because he stinks, having been sweating in the heat, and soon he will hop in the shower to remedy the situation. His stink, as he sees it, is something that can be washed away with a bit of hot water, not like the stink of the "Wogs" and "Pakis," which is somehow inherent, evidence of their repulsive animality. It does not occur to him that Cate wants nothing to do with his penis, because he has just insulted her and everyone she cares about and is generally making a macabre spectacle of himself — death seeps from his pores. Ian does not, apparently, exclude himself from his contempt for humanity, cheerily quipping about how he's slowly killing himself as he chain-smokes and swills gin (he has already had one tar-saturated lung removed and is working steadily on cirrhosis of the liver).

> IAN *opens the door. There is a bottle of gin outside on a tray.*
> IAN *brings it in and stands, unable to decide between gin and champagne*
> CATE: Have champagne, better for you.
> IAN: Don't want it better for me.[18]

Ian projects himself into this future, one in which he is succeeded, devoured by the next generation, he is *spending himself* quickly, too quickly, but there is no joy in his expenditure. Kane's *Phaedra's Love* depicts a Hippolytus who masturbates compulsively and indiscriminately into socks, men, and wom-

---

17 Sarah Kane, *Blasted,* in *Complete Plays* (London: Methuen, 2001), 4, 5, 19.
18 Ibid., 17.

en, including his besotted stepmother Phaedra, without himself experiencing the slightest flicker of pleasure. Ian indulges his vices in much the same way. When he speaks of his children, it is only with bitterness: "Who would have children. You have kids, they grow up, they hate you and you die."[19] Children represent for him an investment without return, with an extra, nihilistic turn of the screw. For Ian, death is the meaning of life, the logical extension of its always-already illogical trajectory.

The first time in *Blasted* when we are given intimations of an alternative way of being is a reference Ian makes to his ex-wife, who apparently left him for another woman, quite probably contributing to some of his vehement aversion to homosexuality. As Ian tells it, "I loved Stella till she became a witch and fucked off with a dyke."[20] As women not dependent upon men, witches, "spinsters," and lesbians are commonly conflated and regarded with suspicion in patriarchal societies. Ian worries intermittently that Cate may have the makings of a lesbian, or as he puts it, a woman capable of "sucking gash."[21] And when he is not worrying about her being too sexual, inappropriately sexual, he is worrying about her not being sexual *enough*. When she rejects his quasi-marriage proposal, he tells her she'll have to leave her Mum one day.

CATE: Why?
IAN: *(Opens his mouth to answer but can't think of one.)*[22]

He can't think of an answer because he is the reason. Ian is the violence of patriarchy personified — bonds between women must be destroyed if he is to survive. Bonds between female lovers are threatening because they remove from circulation two women who ought to have remained active as the currency exchanged between men, and like bonds between mothers and daughters,

19 Ibid., 21.
20 Ibid., 19.
21 Ibid.
22 Ibid., 6.

they are the building blocks of the alliances that could one day challenge the law of the father. In *Gyn/Ecology: The Metaethics of Radical Feminism,* Mary Daly describes the intellectual scaffolding of European witch trials in the fifteenth through eighteenth centuries that claimed the lives of untold hundreds of thousands of women. Daly cites medieval authorities who maintained that "[a]ll witchcraft comes from carnal lust which is in women insatiable."[23] Discussing the practice of female genital mutilation in Africa — where not the whole woman, but only the most offensive part of her is disposed of — Daly argues that infibulation (the most extreme form of clitoridectomy) is in some ways the ultimate expression of a patriarchal obsession with *purity* that cannot countenance a desire as unruly as female desire. Freud believed that women are less adept at sublimation, that is, channeling libidinous energy into "higher" forms of cultural production — they are less discreet, less discrete, and less obsessed with the useful, the productive, and the proprietary. The imbedded value judgment in this assessment has been turned on its head by feminists such as Daly. Cate is also a witch, a Lesbian (which Daly capitalizes to suggest more than a sexual orientation, but a woman who has discovered the power of authentic relationships between women in their myriad forms), and a "spinster" (a woman who has declined to exchange her sex/power for material compensation). Despite the nightmarish paces the play puts him through, the only moment when we see Ian at a real loss is when Cate describes what it feels like when she orgasms. Cate is a kind of holy fool, reminiscent of Dostoevsky's Prince Myshkin in *The Idiot* — both characters experience what appear to be epileptic seizures.

> IAN: When I'm with you I can't think about anything else. You take me to another place.

---

23 Mary Daly, *Gyn/Ecology: The Metaethics of Radical Feminism* (Boston: Beacon Press, 1978), 180, citing Heinrich Kramer and James Sprenger, *The Malleus Maleficarum,* trans. Montague Summers (New York: Cosimo, 2007), 47.

CATE: It's like that when I have a fit.
IAN: Just you.
CATE: The world don't exist, not like this.
   Looks the same but—
   Time slows down.
   A dream I get stuck in, can't do nothing about it.
   One time—
IAN: Make love to me.
CATE: Blocks out everything else.
   Once—
IAN: Make love to you.
CATE: It's like that when I touch myself.
IAN is embarrassed.
CATE: Just before I'm wondering what it'll be like, and just after I'm thinking about the next one, but just as it happens it's lovely, I don't think of nothing else.[24]

Cate exists in an intensely saturated and dangerous patriarchal space throughout the play but ruptures the threadbare tapestry of violence when she reemerges into the ruined space with a baby girl a desperate woman on the outside has entrusted to her care. There is no food, and the baby soon dies, but Cate prays for her:

CATE: Don't feel no pain or know nothing you shouldn't know—
IAN: Cate?
CATE: Shh.
IAN: What are you doing?
CATE: Praying. Just in case.
IAN: Will you pray for me?
CATE: No.
IAN: When I'm dead, not now.
CATE: No point when you're dead.
IAN: You're praying for her.

---

24 Kane, *Blasted*, 22–23

> CATE: She's baby.
> IAN: So?
> CATE: Innocent.
> IAN: Can't you forgive me?
> CATE: Don't see bad things or go bad places —
> IAN: She's dead, Cate.[25]

Ian eats the baby at the end of the play, the grotesque terminus of his mercenary trajectory. He wastes nothing and lays waste to everything. Like a black hole, he devours everything with which he comes into proximity, whereas Cate gives excessively, when nothing is required. They ought to be a perfect match, but they do not share a lexicon; communication is impossible. Ian's "love" for Cate is expressed in terms of brutalization. He tries to manipulate her, shame her into sex, and when she proves intractable, he rapes her. Ian is principally motivated by fear, the heart of capitalism and patriarchy. The two systems share an acquisitive logic, a scarcity mentality even in times of abundance, and a siege mentality even in times of peace. Cate laughs at Ian when he panics and ducks for cover after an engine backfires outside:

> CATE: It's only a car.
> IAN: You. You're fucking thick.
> CATE: I'm not. You're scared of things when there's nothing to be scared of.
> What's thick about not being scared of cars?
> IAN: I'm not scared of cars. I'm scared of dying.
> CATE: A car won't kill you. Not from out there. Not unless you ran out in front of it. *(She kisses him.)* What's scaring you?
> IAN: Thought it was a gun.
> CATE: *(Kisses his neck.)*
> Who'd have a gun?
> IAN: Me.
> CATE: *(Undoes his shirt.)*

25 Ibid., 58.

You're in here.
IAN: Someone like me.[26]

If one assumes that the world is populated by people such as Ian, fear is reasonable. But Cate is a Spinster and as such seeks to cultivate relationships based not on competition, coercion, or recompense but on mutuality, trust, and love freely given without expecting anything in return — or waste, as Ian might call it. In response to Cate's repeated insistence that killing is wrong under any circumstances, Ian scornfully tries to set her straight, "[c]an't always be taking it back down letting them think they've got a right turn the other cheek SHIT some things are worth more than that have to be protected from shit."[27] Such rhetoric has long been a staple of American politics — the conviction that the world is safer when the United States has the most powerful military in the world is recited like an article of faith. Continuing his disquisition on the existential threat posed to America by those Mexicans, Donald Trump argued during presidential debates that "we either have a country, or we don't."[28] After the November 2015 terrorist attacks in Paris, many American governors reacted immediately, announcing that they would refuse to accept any of the Syrian refugees Obama had previously pledged to welcome into the US. The perverse love triangle of *Blasted* would be incomplete without the unnamed darker-skinned soldier who forces his way into Ian and Cate's room, bringing the war with him. In the second part of *Blasted,* the soldier's arrival explodes the form of the play — Ian's insulated world of room service and a victim who can't defend herself is thrown open to the threat of victims turned vindictive, turned more villainous than Ian himself.

The surrealist tone the play takes on when the soldier appears and the fact that he shares no stage time with Cate suggests that

26 Ibid., 28–29.
27 Ibid., 32–33.
28 "Transcript of the Third Debate," *New York Times,* October 20, 2016, https://www.nytimes.com/2016/10/20/us/politics/third-debate-transcript.html.

he is more a phantasm conjured by Ian than a character meant to be seen as possessing an independent existence of his own, the feverish nightmare of a guilt-ridden imperialist who knows that his hour has come. The soldier is an overdetermined figure, the conflation of refugee and terrorist that has become so popular in nationalist discourse. Ian has used the world as his dumping ground, taking for granted that the waste he generates will be disposed of as discreetly and reliably as it is when he flushes the toilet. Žižek describes this type of magical thinking:

> In human dwellings, there is an intermediate space which is disavowed: we all know it exists, but we do not really accept its existence — it remains ignored and (mostly) unsayable. The main content of this invisible space is of course excrement (in the plumbing and sewers), [...] Of course we know well enough how our excrement leaves the house, but our immediate phenomenological relation to it is more radical: it is as if the waste disappears into some netherworld, beyond our sight and out of our world. [...] This is why it is most unpleasant to observe one's excrement coming back up from the pipes into the toilet bowl — something like the return of the living dead.[29]

Like the living dead, the soldier returns, and Ian passes through an exceedingly unpleasant ordeal — the final passages of the play show Ian in tableaux of increasingly extreme abjection. He becomes the most helpless of the helpless cast-offs that he has exploited over his lifetime, ending his life in a pile of rubble, rain pouring down on him through a hole in the ceiling. The luxury hotel becomes a wasteland. The wreckage that has been piling up on the periphery of his life consumes the center. The world that he made is ruined, has ruined him.

---

29 Slavoj Žižek, *Living in the End Times* (New York: Verso, 2011), 259–60.

Charges: Amnesty and the Unforgivable

In "You Bet," the epilogue to *The Merchant's Contracts,* Elfriede Jelinek draws a comparison between the loss of westerners' homes in the 2008 recession and the predicament of the perpetually homeless outsider, the refugee. "No one takes them into their home," Jelinek writes, noting that the westerner who has been exploited by the market is seen as a victim while the foreigner exploited by the market remains an enemy to be feared. He will only bring property values down:

> As much as we try to persuade him, no man would take in strangers, they could kill him, fuck his wife, marry her even, and stay in his house, where the other gets pampered by everyone else here, who now are family to the intruder, the one who wasn't here before. Lost the house he once owned, which is deserted now, vandalized, gutted, who would buy it now? Without pipes, without warmth and water and electricity and sewer connection?, no one will buy something like that and if anyone did, he'd buy another better house, without the poor homeless one in front of the door polluting the air with himself, the dispossessed.[30]

These doubly dispossessed become the subject of Jelinek's *Charges (The Supplicants),* her 2013 play about the European refugee crisis. In *Charges,* Jelinek parodies the discourse of the xenophobe: "[t]hey produce volcanoes of shit and dirt and waste," she writes, "it looks as if a mountain of waste had exploded, go ahead take a look at the mess they make and something like this to live among us now, and for good?"[31]

Subtitling the piece after Aeschylus's drama of that title, Jelinek invokes the chorus of Danaids that functioned as the ancient play's protagonists. In *The Supplicants,* after fleeing forced

---

30 Ibid., 294–95.
31 Elfriede Jelinek, *Charges,* trans. Gitta Honneger (New York: Seagull Books, 2016), 115.

marriage to their Egyptian cousins, the Danaids beg King Pelasgus of Argos for amnesty. They throw themselves at his mercy according to *hiketeia,* a formal custom of supplication that has been called a "ritualization of reciprocity."[32] While the individual being petitioned is not bound to grant the request, a rejection amounts to creating a serious rupture in the fabric of civil society, which is based on the honoring of one's debts. The anthropologist and activist David Graeber proposes that the moral stigma we have become accustomed to attaching to the debtor is at odds with the more fundamental meaning of indebtedness. "Everyday communism," he suggests, is the foundation of all human sociability. Graeber argues that we want and need to incur various kinds of debts and have others be in debt to us; such connections ensure that our relationships have a future.[33] When two friends go out to dinner and one picks up the check, saying, "you get the next one," the friends part ways assuming that there will be a "next one." When two friends go out to dinner and split the check down to the last cent, the friends part ways confident that, should they never see one another again, no one could accuse either of them of defaulting on a financial obligation. Once the ledger is clear, a partnership can be dissolved, but, as Graeber and Aesychlus show, human beings are not built for such radical individualism.

In *The Supplicants,* King Pelasgus initially denies the Danaids protection. He sees them as a potential threat, worrying that they come from the land of the ferocious Amazons. The Danaids attempt to persuade the king that they and he are descended from the same ancestor, but the King remains skeptical. Eventually the Argive people collectively decide to take in the refugees. This appeal to common humanity is central to Jelinek's contemporary revision as well. She picks up on the dominant media language used to describe refugees, the way they are gen-

---

32 John Gould, *Myth, Ritual, Memory, and Exchange: Essays in Greek Literature and Culture* (Oxford: Oxford University Press, 2001), 24.
33 David Graeber, *Debt: The First 5,000 Years* (New York: Melville House Publishing, 2014), 96.

erally referred to as a monolithic, homogenous mass "streaming," "flowing," or "flooding" into the developed world. "The suffering people," she writes "are falling like water off the cliff, down the butte, into the chute, over the mountains, through the sea, over the sea, into the sea, [...] they drown, they crash, they suffocate in cold storage wagons, die in aircraft wheel wells, fall into highway toilets, fall from balconies, yes, people like us!, they are all like us!"[34]

While millions of destitute and endangered African and Middle Eastern people were attempting to secure asylum in Europe, Austria granted citizenship to the opera singer Anna Netrebko and Tatyana Yumesheva, Boris Yeltsin's daughter. Jelinek considers their cases as examples of an unjust system that privileges those with money and influence over those in legitimate need. "We only come in bulk," her chorus of refugees declaims, "no longer individually, never again, even though they pull us out one by one. When will we be somebody again?"[35] The refugees are denied their status as individuals because they can neither pay their way nor barter their commodified celebrity, their hypertrophied individualism. The Austrian state is figured as a for-profit entity as the refugee chorus announces, "[w]e are not value, we are extraneous to the values produced by others, promoted by the corporation."[36] The double meaning of the play's translated title becomes clear as the nature and purpose of debt as Graeber articulates it becomes hopelessly confused: "[t]he whole city bears the guilt [*Schuld*] of our lot," the refugees address the two high-status exiles, "[t]he water bears the guilt, the water carries the debt, bless you both, that you pay me more than the interest, that you pay with your capital, with people who came here as the method of payment for themselves, I'll take them, do you have more of them?"[37] Here the refugees are figured as essentially subsidizing the low-interest "loans" taken

---

34 Jelinek, *Charges*, 15.
35 Ibid., 23.
36 Ibid., 72.
37 Ibid., 38.

out by the likes of Netrebko to gain entry to the country. The most vulnerable members of society seek to become the charges, or wards, of the state, but are instead turned down because of bad credit, so to speak. Their needs are assessed not in terms of what the refugees are owed but in terms of what they will cost.

Graeber asserts that the informal, communitarian ethos of mutually sustaining indebtedness is only replaced by systems of precisely calculated and forcibly collected debts through violent, state intervention. Coinage arose in the first place because warring civilizations could not always trust those they were doing business with to make good on more informal debts and because they had begun ripping people from their social contexts as slaves and needed to find ways to measure the unmeasurable cost of a human life. Refugees also suffer from being ripped from their social contexts, and advanced capitalist nations that might balk at putting a price on an individual human life still engage in cold calculations about lives that "only come in bulk." *Charges* was partly written in response to a 2012 hunger strike staged by refugees housed in the Traiskirchen holding facility near Vienna to protest the living conditions there. Traiskirchen, which the United Nations has described as "inhumane" because of overcrowding, is run by the Swiss firm ORS Service and is representative of an alarming trend toward Western governments adopting the for-profit, private-prison model to address the problem of how to accommodate overwhelming influxes of refugees while saving taxpayers money. This has become a multimillion-dollar industry, with companies charging governments per refugee per night or signing lucrative, multi-year contracts. Many of these operations stand to gain by packing prisoners in and skimping on basic services, but because they are private and not public, they are subject to less oversight, often with disastrous results.[38] Derrida drew on ideas from Levinas and *The Suppliants* when

---

38 Antony Loewenstein, "Private Prisons Are Cashing in on Refugees' Desperation," *New York Times*, February 25, 2016, https://www.nytimes.com/2016/02/25/opinion/private-prisons-are-cashing-in-on-refugees-desperation.html.

he called for progressive urban centers to become "cities of refuge." These places exist. In the US we call them "sanctuary cities," municipalities that decline to enforce cruel federal immigration laws. "Our experience of cities of refuge then," Derrida says, "will not only be that which cannot wait, but something which calls for an urgent response, a just response, [...]. An immediate response to crime, to violence, and to persecution."[39] A fully adequate response will open up a space to reassess notions of nations, borders, democracy, and what it means to be human, to be responsible, and to be in debt to one another.

As was the case when she was writing about the financial crisis in *The Merchant's Contracts,* with *Charges* Jelinek found herself responding to snowballing events in real time, and so was compelled to supplement her original text with appendices. One of these was written after a trio of large-scale catastrophes befell would-be asylum seekers crossing the Mediterranean just during the month of August in 2015. A boat capsized off the coast of Libya, killing two hundred refugees. Fifty went missing shortly after when their rubber dingy sank near the island of Lampedusa. That same week forty were found dead in the hold of a fishing boat that had begun taking on water. Migrants often pay half-price to traverse the Mediterranean below rather than above deck. Commander Massimo Tozzi of the Italian Navy boarded the ship and found the dead bodies in the hold "immersed in water, fuel, and human excrement."[40]

Jelinek seizes on this image, connecting it to the hunger strikers in Vienna and these most recent victims:

> It still must come out, and this end product, which is what becomes of donated meals no one is in charge of, there is nothing and no one, it is a loose end, what's man to do if he

---

39 Jacques Derrida, *On Cosmopolitanism and Forgiveness,* trans. Mark Dooley and Michael Hughes (London: Routledge, 2001), 23.
40 Phillip Pullella, "At Least 40 Migrants Die in Mediterranean: Italian Navy," *Reuters,* August 15, 2015, http://www.reuters.com/article/us-europe-migrants-italy/at-least-40-migrants-die-in-mediterranean-italy-navy-idUSKCN0QK0A320150815.

can't tie ends together, he would have to connect his mouth to his ass, in a sort of short circuit. Oh well, money, shit and the word. If we could spare ourselves these three it would be okay, but unfortunately we have nothing to spare and nothing to save.[41]

The refugees who were protesting in Vienna objected to the poor quality and chaotic distribution of their meals. In Jelinek's text, they are elided with the refugees on the fishing boat; together, they refuse to eat so that they never have to excrete, and therefore will never have to die submerged in their own excrement.

---

41 Jelinek, *Charges*, 128–29.

Epilogue: <u>America</u>

A century after Duchamp's *Fountain*, the Italian artist Maurizio Cattelan installed an eighteen-karat, solid gold toilet in one of the Guggenheim Museum's public restrooms. Titled *America*, the 2016 piece outperforms Duchamp's mass-produced, porcelain model in at least one way; it is fully functional. Visitors to the Guggenheim are permitted and encouraged to literally piss and shit on (well, into) the art object. Cattelan's title seems to single out the United States as the country with the most obscenely bloated art market and general sense of entitlement. Writing for the *Guardian*, a puzzled and distressed Jonathan Jones reacted to the announcement of the installation by opining that

> the real miracle of contemporary art is not that it is bought and sold for lunatic prices by oligarch collectors. It is that you and I also find meaning in it. A luxury object sold for obscene amounts is at the same time a popular phenomenon that draws crowds to galleries. Art is both an investment for the 1% and entertainment for everyone else. If we could understand this paradox we might understand how 21st-century capitalism gets away with so much. […] Can it be that we all buy more deeply into the culture of capitalism than

we acknowledge to ourselves? Perhaps this is a philosophical toilet, after all."[1]

Possibly, some alien species will unearth Cattelan's toilet from the pile of rubble formerly known as the Upper East Side centuries after climate change has sent the East River surging up over FDR Drive, and perhaps the aliens will praise and admire it, as Bataille admired the pyramids of the ancient Egyptians. However, in all likelihood, the wealthy will simply shit in it until it clogs and overflows while teenage boys get shot a couple of miles away in the South Bronx. They'll have to call in a janitor making minimum wage, perhaps someone not so different from the Italian housekeeper who threw Sara Goldschmied and Elenora Chiari's 2015 art installation *Where Are We Going Dancing Tonight?* away, mistaking the installation's materials — empty champagne bottles, cigarette buts, and other evidence of a night of privileged hedonism — for a pile of trash while cleaning up after hours. The janitor will mop up the shit. And that janitor will be the only person who ever understands America.

---

[1] Jonathan Jones, "The Guggenheim's Monstrous Golden Toilet Sums Up the Obscene Art World," *The Guardian,* April 20, 2014, https://www.theguardian.com/artanddesign/jonathanjonesblog/2016/apr/20/maurizio-cattelan-golden-toilet-guggenheim-new-york-duchamp.

Bibliography

"1940s War, Cold War and Consumerism." *Advertising Age,* March 28, 2005. http://adage.com/article/75-years-of-ideas/1940s-war-cold-war-consumerism/102702/.

Adorno, Theodor. *Negative Dialectics.* Translated by E.B. Ashton. New York: The Continuum Publishing Company, 1973.

Aeschylus. "Prometheus Bound." In *Greek Tragedies,* edited by David Grene and Richmond Lattimore, Vol. 1, 61–106. Chicago: University of Chicago Press, 1991.

Al Hussein, Zeid Ra'ad. "Opening Statement and Global Update of Human Rights Concerns by UN High Commissioner for Human Rights Zeid Ra'ad Al Hussein at 38th Session of the Human Rights Council." *United Nations Human Rights Council,* June 18, 2018. https://www.ohchr.org/EN/HRBodies/HRC/Pages/NewsDetail.aspx?NewsID=23206&LangID=E.

Althusser, Louis. *Lenin and Philosophy and Other Essays.* Translated by Ben Brewster. New York: Monthly Review Press, 2001.

Anshelm, Jonas, and Martin Hultman. "A Green Fatwā? Climate Change as a Threat to the Masculinity of Industrial Modernity." NORMA: *International Journal for Masculinity Studies* 9, no. 2 (2014): 84–96. DOI: 10.1080/18902138.2014.908627.

Arendt, Hannah. *The Life of the Mind.* New York: Harcourt, 1971.

Aristotle. *On Poetry and Style.* Translated by G.M.A. Grube. Indianapolis: Hackett, 1989.

Artaud, Antonin. *Antonin Artaud: Selected Writings.* Edited by Susan Sontag. Los Angeles: University of California Press, 1988.

Barney, Matthew. Q&A session following screening of *River of Fundament,* IFC Center, New York, December 6, 2015.

Bataille, Georges. *The Accursed Share.* Translated by Robert Hurley. 3 vols. New York: Zone Books, 1991–92.

———. *The Cradle of Humanity: Prehistoric Art and Culture.* Translated by Stuart Kendall. New York: Zone Books, 2005.

Baudelaire, Charles. *The Essence of Laughter and Other Essays, Journals, and Letters.* Edited by Peter Quennell. New York: Meridian Books, 1956.

Bauman, Zygmunt. *Wasted Lives: Modernity and Its Outcasts.* New York: Polity Press, 2003.

Benhabib, Seyla, Andrei Markovits, and Moishe Postone. "Rainer Werner Fassbinder's *Garbage, the City and Death*: Renewed Antagonisms in the Complex Relationship Between Jews and Germans in the Federal Republic of Germany." *New German Critique* 38 (1986): 3–27. DOI: 10.2307/488073.

Benjamin, Walter. *Illuminations: Essays and Reflections.* Translated by Harry Zorn, edited by Hannah Arendt. New York: Schocken Books, 1969.

Bentley, Eric. *The Life of the Drama.* New York: Athenuem, 1964.

BreakingNews. "Deputy Describes as 'Human Garbage' Syrian Refugees in Europe." *Metatube,* September 13, 2015. https://www.metatube.com/en/videos/284161/Deputy-describes-as-human-garbage-Syrian-refugees-in-Europe/.

Brecht, Bertolt. *The Good Woman of Setzuan.* Translated by Eric Bentley. New York: Grove Press, 1956.

———. *Mother Courage and Her Children.* Translated by Eric Bentley. New York: Grove Press, 1955.

Brooks, Cleanth. *Modern Poetry and the Tradition.* Chapel Hill: University of North Carolina Press, 1939.

Burns, Alexander. "Choice Words from Donald Trump, Presidential Candidate." *New York Times,* June 16, 2015. https://www.nytimes.com/politics/first-draft/2015/06/16/choice-words-from-donald-trump-presidential-candidate/.

Cardwell, Douglas. "The Well-Made Play of Eugène Scribe." *The French Review* 56, no. 6 (1983): 876–84. https://www.jstor.org/stable/392365.

Chaudhuri, Una. "'There Must Be a Lot of Fish in That Lake': Toward an Ecological Theater." *Theater* 25, no. 1 (1994): 23–31. DOI: 10.1215/01610775-25-1-23.

Chekhov, Anton. *Uncle Vanya.* In *The Plays of Anton Chekhov,* translated by Paul Schmidt, 207–56. New York: HarperCollins, 1997.

Cixous, Hélène, and Catherine Clément. "Sorties: Out and Out: Attacks/Ways Out/Forays." In *The Newly Born Woman,* translated by Betsy Wing, 63–134. London: I.B. Tauris, 1996.

Connor, J.D. Lecture in the course "The Art of Disney," Yale University, New Haven, Fall, 2015.

Crutzen, Paul J. "Geology of Mankind." *Nature* 415 (2000): art. 23. DOI: 10.1038/415023a.

Daly, Mary. *Gyn/Ecology: The Metaethics of Radical Feminism.* Boston: Beacon Press, 1978.

Derrida, Jacques. *On Cosmopolitanism and Forgiveness.* Translated by Mark Dooley and Michael Hughes. London: Routledge, 2001.

Descartes, René. *Discourse on Method and Meditations.* New York: The Liberal Arts Press, 1960.

Eliot, T.S. *The Waste Land and Other Poems.* New York: Barnes & Noble Books, 2005.

Eliot, Valerie. *The Letters of T.S. Eliot, Volume I: 1898–1922.* San Diego: Harcourt Brace Jovanovich, 1988.

Fassbinder, Rainer Werner. *Garbage, The City and Death.* In *Plays,* edited by Denis Calandra, 161–89. Baltimore: The Johns Hopkins University Press, 1985.

———. *Katzelmacher.* In *Plays,* edited by Denis Calandra, 75–93. Baltimore: The Johns Hopkins University Press, 1985.

Fausset, Richard. "Refugee Crisis in Syria Raises Fears in South Carolina." *New York Times,* September 25, 2015. https://www.nytimes.com/2015/09/26/us/refugee-crisis-in-syria-raises-fears-in-south-carolina.html.

Fehervary, Helen. "Enlightenment or Entanglement: History and Aesthetics in Bertolt Brecht and Heiner Müller." *New German Critique* 8 (1976): 80–109. DOI: 10.2307/487723.

Freud, Sigmund. "Character and Anal Eroticism." In *The Freud Reader,* edited by Peter Gay, translated by James Strachey, 293–96. New York: Norton & Co., 1989.

———. "Civilization and Its Discontents." In *The Freud Reader,* edited by Peter Gay, translated by James Strachey, 722–71. New York: Norton & Co., 1989.

———. *Three Essays on the Theory of Sexuality.* Edited and translated by James Strachey. New York: Basic Books, 1962.

Fukuyama, Francis. "The End of History?" *The National Interest* 16 (1989): 3–18. https://www.jstor.org/stable/24027184.

Ghosh, Amitav. *The Great Derangement: Climate Change and the Unthinkable.* Chicago: University of Chicago Press, 2016.

Glass, James M. *Life Unworthy of Life: Racial Phobia and Mass Murder in Hitler's Germany.* New York: Basic Books, 1997.

Gold, Matthew K. "The Expert Hand and the Obedient Heart: Dr. Vittoz, T.S. Eliot, and the Therapeutic Possibilities of *The Waste Land.*" *Journal of Modern Literature* 23, nos. 3–4 (Summer 2000): 519–33. DOI: 10.1353/jml.2000.0007.

Goldstein, Bill. *The World in Two: Virginia Woolf, T.S. Eliot, D.H. Lawrence, E.M. Forster, and the Year That Changed Literature.* New York: Henry Holt, 2017.

Gould, John. *Myth, Ritual, Memory, and Exchange: Essays in Greek Literature and Culture.* Oxford: Oxford University Press, 2001.

Graeber, David. *Debt: The First 5,000 Years*. New York: Melville House Publishing, 2014.

Granville-Barker, Harley. *The Voysey Inheritance*. Boston: Little, Brown, and Company, 1916.

———. *Waste*. In *Three Plays: The Marrying off Ann Leete, The Voysey Inheritance, Waste*, 214–351. London: Sidgwick & Jackson, 1909.

Gueullette, Thomas-Simon. "Le Marchand du Merde." In *Theatre des Boulevards, ou recueil de parades*, edited by A. Mahon, 237–60. Paris: De l'imprimerie de Gilles Langlois, 1756.

Haraway, Donna. *Staying with the Trouble: Making Kin in the Chthulucene*. Durham: Duke University Press, 2016.

Hay, Eloise Knapp. *T.S. Eliot's Negative Way*. Cambridge: Harvard University Press, 1982.

Hewitt, Margaret. *Wives and Mothers in Victorian Industry*. London: Rockliff, 1958.

Hirschfeld Davis, Julie, Sheryl Gay Stolberg, and Thomas Kaplan. "Trump Alarms Lawmakers with Disparaging Words for Haiti and Africa." *New York Times*, January 11, 2018. https://www.nytimes.com/2018/01/11/us/politics/trump-shithole-countries.html.

"Holoscenes." *The Times Square Arts*. http://www.timessquarenyc.org/times-square-arts/projects/at-the-crossroads/holoscenes/index.aspx.

Honegger, Gitta. "Introduction." In Elfriede Jelinek, *Rechnitz and The Merchant's Contracts*, 1–62. New York: Seagull Books, 2015.

Hume, Robert, trans. *The Thirteen Principal Upanishads*. London: Oxford University Press, 1921.

Ibsen, Henrik. *An Enemy of the People*. In *Four Major Plays*, Vol. 2, translated by Rolf Fjelde, 83–198. New York: Penguin Books, 1970.

———. *John Gabriel Borkman*. In *Four Major Plays*, Vol. 2, translated by Rolf Fjelde, 307–96. New York: Penguin Books, 1970.

IPCC. "Summary for Policymakers." In *Global Warming of 1.5°C,* https://www.ipcc.ch/sr15/chapter/spm/.

Isherwood, Charles. "An Ibsen Who Rages over Ritalin and Economic Austerity Plans." *New York Times,* November 7, 2013. https://www.nytimes.com/2013/11/08/theater/reviews/a-contemporary-enemy-of-the-people-at-the-harvey-theater.html.

Jameson, Fredric. "Culture and Finance Capital." *Critical Inquiry* 24, no. 1 (1997): 246–65. DOI: 10.1086/448873.

Jelinek, Elfriede. *Bambiland. Theater* 39, no. 3 (2009): 111–43. DOI: 10.1215/01610775-2009-008.

———. *Charges.* Translated by Gitta Honegger. New York: Seagull Books, 2016.

———. "I Am a *Trümmerfrau* of Language." *Theater* 36, no. 2 (2006): 20–37. DOI: 10.1215/01610775-36-2-20.

———. *Princess Plays: Jackie. Theater* 36, no. 2 (2006): 53–65. DOI: 10.1215/01610775-36-2-52.

———. *Rechnitz and The Merchant's Contracts.* Translated by Gitta Honegger. New York: Seagull Books, 2015.

———"Sidelined." Lecture presented to the Nobel Prize Summit at the Swedish Academy, Stockholm, Sweden, December 7, 2004. Translated by Martin Chalmers. http://www.nobelprize.org/nobel_prizes/literature/laureates/2004/jelinek-lecture-e.html.

———. *Sports Play.* Translated by Penny Black. London: Oberon Books, 2012.

Jones, Jonathan. "The Guggenheim's Monstrous Golden Toilet Sums Up the Obscene Art World," *The Guardian,* April 20, 2014. https://www.theguardian.com/artanddesign/jonathanjonesblog/2016/apr/20/maurizio-cattelan-golden-toilet-guggenheim-new-york-duchamp.

Kalb, Jonathan. *The Theater of Heiner Müller.* New York: Limelight Editions, 2001.

Kane, Sarah. *Blasted.* In *Complete Plays,* 1–61. London: Methuen Drama, 2001.

Kant, Immanuel. *Critique of Judgment.* Translated by J.H. Bernard. London: Macmilland & Co., 1914.

Kerr, Walter. "The Love between Beckett and Actors Isn't Mutual." *New York Times,* November 13, 1988. https://www.nytimes.com/1988/11/13/theater/stage-view-the-love-between-beckett-and-actors-isn-t-mutual.html.

Klein, Naomi. *No Logo: Taking Aim at Brand Bullies.* New York: Picador, 2000.

Knight, Christopher. "Mathew Barney's 'River of Fundament'? Well, It's Certainly Big." *Los Angeles Times,* September 26, 2015. https://www.latimes.com/entertainment/arts/museums/la-ca-cm-knight-barney-review-20150927-column.html.

Kolbert, Elizabeth. *The Sixth Extinction: An Unnatural History.* New York: Henry Holt and Company, 2014.

Kramer, Heinrich, and Sprenger, James. *The Malleus Maleficarum.* Translated by Montague Summers. New York: Cosimo, 2007.

Kristeva, Julia. *Powers of Horror: An Essay on Abjection.* Translated by Leon S. Roudiez. New York: Columbia University Press, 1982.

Lacan, Jacques. *On Feminine Sexuality: The Limits of Love and Knowledge.* Translated by Bruce Fink. New York: Norton, 1998.

Lears, T.J. Jackson. *No Place of Grace: Anti-Modernism and the Transformation of American Culture 1880–1920.* New York: Pantheon, 1981.

"Lebenslange Haft für fünffachen Axtmörder" ["Life Sentence for Five-Time Ax Murderer"]. *Spiegel Online,* November 7, 2008. https://www.spiegel.de/panorama/justiz/wien-lebenslange-haft-fuer-fuenffachen-axtmoerder-a-589185.html.

Leggett, Jane A. "Potential Implications of U.S. Withdrawal from the Paris Agreement on Climate Change." *Congressional Research Service,* April 5, 2019. https://crsreports.congress.gov/product/pdf/IF/IF10668.

Lehmann, Hans-Thies. *Postdramatic Theatre.* Translated by Karen Jürs-Munby. New York: Routledge, 2006.

Levinas, Emmanuel. *Otherwise Than Being*. Translated by Alphonso Lingis. Dordrecht: Springer Science and Business Media, 1991.

Loewenstein, Antony. "Private Prisons Are Cashing in on Refugees' Desperation." *New York Times,* February 25, 2016. https://www.nytimes.com/2016/02/25/opinion/private-prisons-are-cashing-in-on-refugees-desperation.html.

Mailer, Norman. *Ancient Evenings*. Boston: Little Brown, 1983.

"Maldives Government Highlights the Impact of Climate Change — By Meeting Underwater." *Daily Mail,* October 20, 2009. http://www.dailymail.co.uk/news/article-1221021/Maldives-underwater-cabinet-meeting-held-highlight-impact-climate-change.html.

Mannex, Colin. "Preface to Elfriede Jelinek's *Bambiland*." *Theater* 39, no. 3 (2009): 107–9. DOI: 10.1215/01610775-2009-007.

Marcuse, Herbert. *Eros and Civilization: A Philosophical Inquiry into Freud*. Boston: Beacon Press, 1955.

Marranca, Bonnie. *Ecologies of Theater: Essays at the Century Turning*. Baltimore: Johns Hopkins University Press, 1996.

Marx, Karl. *Capital*. Vol. 1. Translated by Ben Fowkes. New York: Penguin, 1976.

———. "On the Jewish Question." In *The Marx–Engels Reader,* edited by Robert C. Tucker, 26–52. New York: Norton, 1978.

"Mass Murder as Party Entertainment?" *Der Spiegel,* October 22, 2007. https://www.spiegel.de/international/germany/historians-dispute-journalist-s-claims-mass-murder-as-party-entertainment-a-512869.html.

McKenzie, Jon. *Perform or Else: From Discipline to Performance*. New York: Routledge, 2001.

Miller, Arthur. *Death of a Salesman*. New York: Dramatists Play Service, 1948.

Millet, Kate. *Sexual Politics*. New York: Columbia University Press, 1969.

Moore, Jason W. *Anthropocene or Capitalocene? Nature, History, and the Crisis of Capitalism*. Oakland: PM Press, 2016.

Morton, Timothy. *Hyperobjects: Philosophy and Ecology after the End of the World.* Minneapolis: University of Minnesota Press, 2013.

Müller, Heiner, *Hamletmachine and Other Texts for the Stage,* edited and translated by Carl Weber. Baltimore: The Johns Hopkins University Press, 1984.

———. *Mauser.* In *A Heiner Müller Reader: Plays, Poetry, Prose,* edited and translated by Carl Weber, 93–107. Baltimore: Johns Hopkins University Press, 2001.

Næss, Arne. *Ecology, Community and Lifestyle: Outline of an Ecosophy.* Translated by David Rothenberg. Cambridge: Cambridge University Press, 1989.

Nietzsche, Friedrich. *On the Use and Abuse of History for Life.* Translated by Adrian Collins. New York: Cosimo, 2005.

Nixon, Ron. "Food Waste Is Becoming Serious Economic and Environmental Issue, Report Says." *New York Times,* February 25, 2015. https://www.nytimes.com/2015/02/26/us/food-waste-is-becoming-serious-economic-and-environmental-issue-report-says.html.

Perelman, Michael. *Transcending the Economy: On the Potential of Passionate Labor and the Wastes of the Market.* New York: Palgrave, 2000.

Pullella, Phillip. "At Least 40 Migrants Die in Mediterranean: Italian Navy." *Reuters,* August 15, 2015. http://www.reuters.com/article/us-europe-migrants-italy/at-least-40-migrants-die-in-mediterranean-italy-navy-idUSKCN0QK0A320150815.

Raitt, Suzanne. "Psychic Waste: Freud, Fechner, and the Principle of Constancy." In *Culture and Waste: The Creation and Destruction of Value,* edited by Gay Hawkins and Stephen Muecke, 73–83. New York: Rowman & Littlefield Publishers, 2002.

@realDonaldTrump (Donald J. Trump). *Twitter,* November 6, 2012, 2:15pm. https://twitter.com/realDonaldTrump/status/265895292191248385.

———. *Twitter,* January 29, 2014, 1:27am. https://twitter.com/realDonaldTrump/status/428414113463955457.

Scanlan, John. *On Garbage.* London: Reaktion Books, 2005.

Schlaich, Frieder. *Christoph Schlingensief and His Films.* Berlin: Filmgalerie 451, 2005.

Schlipphacke, Heidi M. *Nostalgia after Nazism: History, Home, and Affect in German and Austrian Literature and Film.* Lewisburg: Bucknell University Press, 2010.

Shakespeare, William. *Hamlet.* In *The Norton Shakespeare,* edited by Stephen Greenblatt, 1696–784. New York: Norton, 2008.

———. *The Tempest.* Edited by Stanley Wells et al. New York: Penguin Books, 2007.

Shawn, Wallace. *Evening at the Talk House.* New York: Theatre Communications Group, 2017.

———. *The Fever.* New York: Grove Press, 1991.

———. *Grasses of a Thousand Colors.* New York: Theatre Communications Group, 2014.

———. "The Art of Theater No. 17." Interview by Hilton Als, *The Paris Review* 201 (2012). https://www.theparisreview.org/interviews/6154/wallace-shawn-the-art-of-theater-no-17-wallace-shawn.

Simon, John. "Waste." *New York Magazine,* March 27, 2000. https://nymag.com/nymetro/arts/theater/reviews/2487/.

Steiner, George. *The Death of Tragedy.* New Haven: Yale University Press, 1996.

Teresa of Ávila. *Book of My Life.* Translated by Mirabai Starr. Boston: New Seeds Books, 2007.

Thatcher, Margaret. "AIDS, Education and the Year 2000!" Interview by Douglas Keay, *Woman's Own* (October 31, 1987).

Tolstoy, Leo. *What Is Art?* Translated by Richard Pevear and Larissa Volokhonsky. New York: Penguin Books, 1995.

"Transcript of the Third Debate." *New York Times,* October 20, 2016. https://www.nytimes.com/2016/10/20/us/politics/third-debate-transcript.html.

Verdoner, Yoka. "Nazis Separated Me from My Parents as a Child. The Trauma Lasts a Lifetime." *The Guardian,* June 18, 2018. https://www.theguardian.com/commentisfree/2018/

jun/18/separation-children-parents-families-us-border-trump.

Viney, William. *Waste: A Philosophical History of Things.* London: Bloomsbury Academic, 2014.

Wirth, Andrzej, and Marta Ulvaeus. "The Lehrstück as Performance." TDR: *The Drama Review* 43, no. 4 (1999): 113–21. DOI: 10.1162/105420499760263570.

Žižek, Slavoj. *Living in the End Times.* New York: Verso, 2011.

www.ingramcontent.com/pod-product-compliance
Lightning Source LLC
Chambersburg PA
CBHW072046160426
43197CB00014B/2649